D0480919

FULL TO THE BUNG!

by Duncan Gillespie

A bedside book for
winemakers, beermakers and Kofyars!

Cover and Cartoons by Rex Royle and Stan Baker

© THE AMATEUR WINEMAKER

SBN 0 900841 35 4

Printed in Great Britain by
Standard Press (Andover) Ltd., South Street, Andover, Hants.
Telephone 2413

CONTENTS

CHAPTER ONE

OPENING SHOTS

Better Customer

Bottling of one's own wine, so far from injuring the wine merchants, is more likely to help them. A man who bottles some wine for himself (as you will find, I should warn you) doesn't buy less wine outside. He buys more. He gets in the habit of wine-drinking and wine-comparing. He must have other wines to go with it, and contrast with it. He is in fact a better customer than before. More choosey and more intelligent, I admit; but that the merchants must put up with.

RAYMOND POSTGATE.

★ ★ ★

The dipsomaniac and the abstainer both make the same mistake: they both regard wine as a drug and not as a drink.

G. K. CHESTERTON.

★ ★ ★

Born Shouting

Every child born into the world opens its mouth to shout before it opens its eyes to see. It shouts for a drink, and it gets it. It becomes a habit, one which many men never lose. Even when there is drink enough in their own homes, they cannot resist the urge to go where they can shout for it, to an inn or a pub.

ANDRE SIMON. DRINK.

"*Hic! nushing to declare*"

Proud

We winemakers have not the slightest reason to be apologetic about our products, and most of them compare very favourably indeed with the ordinary wines of the Continent. Some of our wines may be far from first class, but there are indifferent wines on the Continent as well, you know. . . . Buy, a glass of ordinary cheap red wine in your "local"—and see if you don't prefer your own elderberry!

What we tend to forget is that it is the better foreign wines which are exported, the "ordinary" ones stay in their country of origin as a rule. Far from being ashamed of our wines, I think we should be proud of the high standard we, *as amateurs*, have attained nationally, and certainly the enthusiastic amateur winemaker in this country tends to amass an even wider knowledge of the subject than the French or German countryman, who may have been making wine in quantities for years, but who does so by traditional methods and has never bothered to study the whys and wherefores of the subject.

C. J. J. BERRY, IN A.W.

★　★　★

Wine was created from the beginning to make men joyful and not to make them drunk.

ECCLESIASTICUS, CH. XXXI

★　★　★

Drink wine in winter for cold and in summer for heat.

OLD PROVERB.

"*Take me to your leader*"

The difference between beer and wine is that beer makes a man feel that he has married the right woman, whereas wine makes him feel quite certain that he has.

QUOTED IN A.W.

★　★　★

Better than Jam

Beer was brewed quarterly in cottages and once a month in the richer houses. Fruit wines were made as each ingredient came into season and such wines became an important part of the household pharmacopoeia, their medicinal qualities understood and highly appreciated. Celery wine was used against gout and rheumatism, Cowslip an antidote for insomnia, Elderberry wine was a remedy against coughs and colds in winter, Herb wines a carminative, and Parsnip wine respected as a laxative.

The knowledge of baking and brewing became an essential part of a girl's education. As wives they were in charge of those duties, except in households where the men looked after the drinks. . . . The Elizabethan housewife made wine far more commonly than she made jam. Jam was for children, like sweets.

ANDRE LAUNAY: EAT, DRINK AND BE SORRY.

★　★　★

THE WINEMAKER'S BLESSING

May your ferments keep frothing and foaming
Till the alcohol content is high;
May you never have recourse to fining
May your siphon tubes never run dry!　　A.W.

Circles and Guilds

The first Winemakers' Circle in the country was formed at Andover, in Hampshire, in January 1954, as a result of some recipes for home-brewed beer which had been published in the local newspaper's Christmas Supplement. . . . At Andover the name "Circle" was chosen, as typifying the friendliness and compactness it was hoped to foster; elsewhere the title "Guild" was preferred, as being particularly applicable to a skilled craft.

Fundamentally, the Circles are certainly similar to the ancient Guilds in that they include those whose knowledge and experience would rate them the rank of a master winemaker. There are many with sufficient experience to rate them journeymen and there are many coming forward as apprentices. Furthermore, as of old, the purposes of the Guilds are to keep alive this country's tradition of wine-making, to assist their members to improve the standard of their craft and to help beginners.

TURNER AND BERRY: THE WINEMAKER'S COMPANION.

★ ★ ★

"Were the art of brewing" continues Mr. Booth, "generally understood, the trade of a public brewer could exist only upon the earnings of the poor, for all who could muster a few pounds would brew for themselves".

THE WORSHIP OF BACCHUS A GREAT DELUSION; 1876

In Conclave

It's some years now since I last went as an observer to a national amateur wine-making conference. . . . Nearly 2000 bottles of wine had been entered for judging in the 42 different classes and they varied in colour from urine gold to cough mixture pink. I saw bottles of Indian tea, primrose, passion fruit, birch sap, oak leaf, clover, rose petal, clementine, artichoke, and nettle tip alongside the more everyday varieties such as apple, plum, cherry, damson, rhubarb, gooseberry, blackcurrant and potato.

Winemakers in conclave are a jolly lot, very proud of their ancient mystery, the little miracle by which a bucketful of foul-looking fruit and veg. can be transformed into liquid sunshine. Each winemaker usually brings a couple of his best bottles to the lunch so no one goes thirsty. Sitting next to me at one of these lunches a Pickwickian old solicitor exchanged wines with his neighbour. "You try that nettle" he beamed "You'll find it very nice and nutty". At another table a red-faced gentleman was appraising a glass of what looked like Arbois. He inhaled the bouquet, sipped a little, and a smile broke over his face: "Bless my soul, you can smell the roses in this; what a breath of summer!"

COOPER: BEVERAGE REPORT.

★ ★ ★

Taken socially in small-to-moderate amounts . . . alcohol is one of mankind's happiest discoveries. But taken uncontrollably in larger amounts, alcohol is certainly the curse that many teetotallers think it.

DR. BRADSHAW: THE DRUGS YOU TAKE.

CHAPTER TWO

MATCH THOSE!

�֍

Delicate

"The cowslip, delicate and silky to the palate; the ginger, full of flavour and of body; the red-currant, rich and sweet—a lady's wine; the gooseberry, possessing all the finer qualities of the grape of Epernay; the raisin with fine Tokay flavour; or the raspberry, full of bouquet and of beeswing".

SIR WALTER BESANT, 1888.

★ ★ ★

Balanced

Good champagne has an incomparably fresh and delicate taste of grapes. There is hardly any sugar in it at all, but just enough to balance a slight acidity— the perfect balance of, say, a crisp golden-green apple. It has an extraordinarily pungent smell—you can smell a bottle being opened in the next garden— and yet the scent in the top of your glass is as delicate and fresh as the wine itself. Finally, it has a perfect mill-race of pin-point bubbles, slowly settling down to gently racing streamers from the bottom of the glass. The total effect of the wine is one of richness, belying the fact that it is completely dry, and never, at least in my experience, cloys.

HUGH JOHNSON. WINE.

"*I said you were putting in too much flaming nutriment!*"

High Flown

"The peace of a sunset, the warmth and scents of a summer evening, the soft caress of strong and sensitive fingers" applied to the 1953 Chateau Lafite may seem high flown, but at least it is a description of the impressions made on the taster in terms that can be understood.

ALLAN SICHEL: PENGUIN BOOK OF WINES.

★ ★ ★

Velvet Depth Charge

Russian Stout is about twice as strong as Guinness, half as strong again as Bass Barley Wine, and the nip is said to pack the same alcoholic punch as four whiskies. They told me at the cellars that nobody had ever floored four at one go and not shown the effects. A smooth rich velvety depth-charge of a drink— sweet, but with the sweetness only of the malt, for there is no added sugar, and yet with the bitter tang of hops.

CYRIL RAY: IN A GLASS LIGHTLY.

★ ★ ★

Garden of Flowers

Kientzheim is a little village in Alsace and the muscat from there—made with the muscat grape—smells like a garden of flowers.

T. A. LAYTON: WINE'S MY LINE.

"*Made that beer a bit strong didn't you?*
—I just used some as a shampoo"

Summer in a Glass

We swirled it in our glasses and found it so hard to disentangle the sunshiny colour and the apple-blossom fragrance from the honeyish grapey sweetness and the crisp, almost lemony acidity in the mouth that we might have been drinking sunshine and listening to apple-blossom. Here was that famous summer of 1959 in a glass.

CYRIL RAY (describing a German trockenbeerenaus-
lese of 1959).

★ ★ ★

All Wine

"Think, for a moment, of an almost paper-white glass of liquid, just shot with greeny-gold, just tart on your tongue, full of wild-flower scents and spring-water freshness. And think of a burnt-umber fluid, as smooth as syrup in the glass, as fat as butter to smell, and sea-deep with strange flavours. Both are wine."

Wine is grape-juice. Every drop of liquid filling so many bottles has been drawn out of the ground by the roots of a vine. All these different drinks have at one time been sap in a stick. It is the first of many strange and some—despite modern research—mysterious circumstances which go to make wine not only the most delicious, but the most fascinating, drink in the world. HUGH JOHNSON: WINE.

"Extra dry — it was a hot snmmer"

Tarpaulin and Lace

His descriptions of wines can be vivid. Like wet wool. A balance of hard and gentle, flowery and strong; an almost claret-like delicacy and an irresistible raspberry-like scent; tarpaulin edged with lace; velvety, peachlike and penetrating; frivolous as flowers; apple-like freshness and bite, a marvellous mingling of honey in the scent and steel in the finish.
HUGH JOHNSON'S "WORLD ATLAS OF WINE",

QUOTED IN A.W.

★ ★ ★

Smooth

Sir, I have now in my cellar ten tun of the best ale in Staffordshire; 'tis smooth as oil, sweet as milk, clear as amber, and strong as brandy; and will be just fourteen year old the fifth day of next March. . .
THE BEAUX STRATAGEM.

CHAPTER THREE

GEEYUCH!

Catty

It has been said of the English that they can make wine out of anything—except grapes. Personally, I prefer cowslip wine and loganberry wine; but different wines appeal to different people. Edith was in the scullery, in our early days, when she heard the two young girls in the kitchen enjoying one of their interminable dull conversations while they worked. Elderflower wine was mentioned.

Said one "Have you ever tasted that?"
"Yes".
"What do that taste like?"
"That taste of cat's pee and pepper".
"I reckon I shouldn't like that".
"Oh, that's good, that is. My Aunt Beat give me that when I go there Sundays".

J. AND E. B. ROOKE: SUFFOLK PROSPECT.

★ ★ ★

I think I preferred it to some sparkling Lacrima Christi, which suggested ginger beer alternatively stirred with a stick of chocolate and a large sulphur match.   GEORGE SAINTSBURY.

★ ★ ★

It was somewhere between Genoa and Turin that my wife and I stopped one very hot day and went into a little wineshop in a village to fill our two-litre flask with local wine. . . . We filled the flask and then had a glass each; it tasted very strongly of raspberry syrup in which a rather old tom-cat had been steeped.   EDWARD HYAMS IN "WINE MINE".

"*It has a distinct mousey flavour*"

Spit in the Basin

This is a most peculiar procedure in which the beauty of young maidens, selected for their rosy lips and white teeth, is supposed to counteract the unappetising method of making the brew. The chosen girls (always unmarried) wear hibiscus flowers tucked in their long dark hair, but little else, as they sit in groups of four or five around ornately carved wooden bowls with piles of the snarled roots beside them. They are obliged to chew these into a soft mass, taking care not to swallow in the process.

The quids are deposited in the bowls and stirred by hand until the liquid portion takes on the appearance of milky soap suds, which is then strained through a sieve made of narrow strips of bark before being passed around in a communal cup to the guests. Because it tends to destroy the teeth of the industrious chewers, this traditional method of making kava is being abandoned. But it does not seem to be a source of infection, despite its unhygienic manufacture. Possibly it contains a self-purifying or antibiotic property.

In the modern method of preparation, the roots are pounded between two stones, rather than masticated by virgins.

This is said to produce a far less potent drink, and one actually quite different in its action.

M. B. Kreig: Green Medicine.

★ ★ ★

Gallows Wine—Humorous reference to a German wine so harsh and strong that after it has been drunk the gallows are unnecessary—because, they say, the Galgenwein trickling down the throat of the drinker can choke him so effectively that no gallows rope is needed.

Lichine: Encyclopaedia of Wines and Spirits.

Surplus

The most notorious area on the way is the dull flat country west of the Rhone delta. There is a constant surplus of bad red wine in this area. The growers are given to striking and picketing if the government does not do something to help them to get rid of it. Sometimes the government distils it to make industrial alcohol, sometimes it gets the army to drink it (at other times, when there has been a milk surplus, the long-suffering army has been switched over to milk). HUGH JOHNSON. WINE.

★   ★   ★

Apart from its aphrodisiac action, too much kava paralyses the legs, leaving the head clear.

DR. BERNARD FINCH: PASSPORT TO PARADISE?

★   ★   ★

Applejack (distilled cider). That the product was powerful is proved by the way it was referred to in the local taverns, where customers would ask for "A slug of blue fish-hooks", "essence of lock-jaw", or, after the centre of the trade had moved to New Jersey, for "Jersey Lightning".

LICHINE. ENCYCLOPAEDIA OF WINES AND SPIRITS.

25

The Real Maguey

The yield of a birch-tree is measured in pints, the Maguey cactus in Mexico will yield a gallon of sap a day—it wells up into the cavity left when the central stem is cut across and hollowed out. A single plant, it seems, gives a ton of juice before it dies. The juice is sweet and acid, due to fructose and malic acid—it seems a tempting proposition for the Mexican wine-maker. But he ferments it in large vats made of leather and it ends up tasting of sour butter or putrid meat . . .

QUOTED IN A.W.

Nailed

I reluctantly chewed my way through a glassful of two-year-old elderberry this morning, a small diversion during a shopping tour, and wasn't a bit surprised to hear that there were 7 lb. to the gallon in it. If I had been told that there was plus two pounds of rusty nails I would have believed it. The tannin left me with an uncomfortable mouth until I could get to a glass of milk.

THE LATE CHERRY LEEDS IN A.W.

Then, when we had finished the bottle, a couple of the others suggested that we each chip in and go out to buy another bottle of wine. "Oh no" I joked. "Let's just chip in a dollar apiece and I'll bring up five dollar's worth of my wine".

My "friend" said, "The six of us couldn't carry five dollars' worth of your wine".

ROGER L. WELSH IN A.W.

CHAPTER FOUR

WORTH KNOWING

Do's and dont's of Winemaking

Do use sound fruit.

Don't forget to wash your fruit.

Do boil your fruit, or add one or two Campden tablets if your fruit is over-ripe or unsound.

Don't use metal containers for fermenting.

Do remember to sterilise wooden containers.

Don't forget to wash all utensils.

Do remember to use the right amount of sugar.

Don't forget to test the gravity of the adjusted juice.

Do remember that the gravity of fruit juices varies.

Don't forget to use a suitable wine yeast.

Do remember to add a yeast nutrient to fruit wines.

Do remember to cover your fermenter during pulp fermentation.

Do insert a fermentation trap.

Don't fill your container full until the first vigorous fermentation has subsided.

Do remember to have some spare wine for filling up.

Don't allow an air space over any wine during secondary fermentation and maturing, with the exception of sherry.

Do give sherry wine plenty of air.

Don't forget that flower wines need fruit juice.

Do remember to add acid where necessary.

Don't add sugar in the solid state, always dissolve in fruit juice or water.

Do remember that adding sugar or syrup at intervals makes for stronger wines.

Don't forget to rack your wines at intervals.

Do top up your fermenter after racking, with water if no spare wine is available.

Don't fine your wine unless it refuses to clarify after several rackings.

Do stir up the wine yeast to help your wine to clarify.

Don't forget that racking improves wine flavour.

Do remember that wines are stabilised by racking.

Don't bottle your wine until it has been tested for stability.

Do remember to add one or more Campden tablets to wines which darken on standing.

Don't add a Campden tablet to wine which is to become sherry.

Do remember wine making requires patience.

Don't despair, even poor wines improve on maturing.

S. M. TRITTON: AMATEUR WINE MAKING.

A sprightly old vicar named Mont
Fermented his wine in the font
When asked why he did it
Said "When put in the pulpit
It runs through the holes in the front".

MARY EDRICH, BURY ST. EDMUNDS.

There was a young fellow called Knox
Who filtered his wine through his socks,
His friend said "Old sport
You have ruined this port,
You should only use socks on your hocks".

F. GILBERT, EVESHAM, IN A.W.

Cook with Wine

Apart from the obvious advantage of the flavour profile of a dish cooked or prepared with wine, what other reasons are there for using wine in cooking? I am sure no-one will deny that psychologically it is right—how much nicer it is to add wine rather than water to a casserole, for example, and who will deny that any recipe which says "Add a glass of red wine" has an appeal of its own, and conjures up thoughts of a superb dish, seeming to be synonymous with adding quality to a dish . . .

When wine is used to cook fish or meat, the wine and juices from the food may be used to form the basis of a sauce, so all the goodness is put back into the dish and nothing is wasted or thrown away. If meat is "roasted" in wine instead of fat, or cooked in wine in a casserole dish with a lid, less shrinkage is apparent and the juices may be thickened or reduced by fast boiling to give a rich satisfying "gravy".

TILLY TIMBRELL, AUTHOR OF "THE WINEMAKER'S COOKBOOK" AND "THE WINEMAKER'S DINING BOOK", WRITING IN A.W.

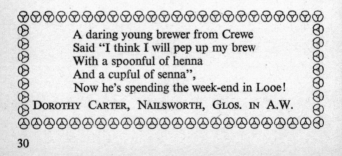

A daring young brewer from Crewe
Said "I think I will pep up my brew
With a spoonful of henna
And a cupful of senna",
Now he's spending the week-end in Looe!

DOROTHY CARTER, NAILSWORTH, GLOS. IN A.W.

"*Why in the blazes did you have to carry that recipe book about with you, pet?*"

Basic

The process of fermentation, which is what is happening when the yeast cells get to work, produces turbulent eruptions in the juice. Not only alcohol is made, but carbon dioxide gas is given off in large quantities. Its bubbles keep the mass of broken grapes moving. At the same time the heat given off by the reaction makes it warm.

Fermentation goes on until the sugar supply runs out, or until the yeast cells are asphyxiated by the growing concentration of alcohol, whichever happens sooner. Usually it is the sugar which gives out first. The liquid, then, instead of being a solution of sugar and water, is a solution of alcohol in water, with the same small quantities of the acids and oils which give it its peculiar flavour and scent. On an average there will be about 10 per cent of alcohol in red wine, a little more—11 or so—in white. There is no sugar left at all, and the wine is completely dry.

If, on the other hand, the grapes were so ripe that there was still more sugar to ferment when a concentration of 15 per cent alcohol was reached, it would be the yeast cells which would give out first. In a solution of alcohol this strong they grow drowsy and cease to function, they are not dead, but they are completely under the table. When this happens there is still some sugar left unconverted into alcohol, and the wine is more or less sweet to the taste.

This process is the basic one for the making of all wine and, come to that, of any other alcoholic drink.

HUGH JOHNSON: WINE.

★　★　★

Too much air above wine can be harmful. In a storage jar the amount of air can be reduced by simply dropping in glass marbles which have been sterilised.

G. H. SLADE, HIGH WYCOMBE, IN A.W.

Archie's Find

It was the Greek Archimedes, who in the 3rd century B.C. found that a solid, wholly or partly immersed in a liquid undergoes an apparent loss of weight, which loss equals the weight of fluid that is displaced. It seems that Archie, as we called him affectionately or derisively at school, discovered this principle while having a bath, and was so excited that he ran down the High Street shouting "I've got it!" in fluent Greek, but as nudes were then ten a drachma, presumably no-one bothered too much. . . .

It is easy to see from this how the hydrometer functions, as it is weighted at the bottom of the elongated bulb, it floats in an upright position with the bulb immersed and part of the stem projecting above the surface. The reading is taken where the liquid cuts across the stem. If the liquid's density is high, as it is when it contains a proportion of unfermented sugar, the upthrust is stronger, and consequently more of the stem projects. . . . As the sugar is fermented out, so the liquid's density decreases and accordingly the upthrust is less; this causes the hydrometer to sink lower, and the reading given this time will be below the former one and nearer the top of the stem.

CEDRIC AUSTIN: WHYS AND WHEREFORES OF WINE-
MAKING.

★ ★ ★

Elderberry stains seem to resist all attempts to remove them. Readers may be interested to know that I was able to remove the stained area of my shirt by soaking it overnight in a solution of 1 teaspoonful of Silana p.f. and half a pint of warm water.

DAVID SMITH, DEVON, IN A.W.

Think Big

Sooner or later, most winemakers are not content to make just one gallon of their favourite wines: their thoughts turn to the idea of making them in larger quantities, say $4\frac{1}{2}$, 5 or 6 gallons, or even more.

Many winemakers make 20 or 30 gallons of their favourite wine each year, and this "bulk" method has much to commend it. Many winemakers are nervous of attempting, say, 5 gallons of one wine, but it is a fact that 5 gallons is much less likely to "go wrong" than one, if ordinary precautions are observed.

. . . By making a few wines in bulk you can have as much wine to drink as you wish, every day . . . a satisfying thought.

The way to set about it is to choose one or two ingredients which are readily available, or very cheap, and which can be relied upon to give you a wine of reasonable quality for your vin ordinaire, both red and white.

I personally have settled for apple for the white (from which a whole range of wines can be produced) and dried bilberry for the red.

C. J. J. BERRY: FIRST STEPS IN WINEMAKING.

★ ★ ★

No Romance

It is all very romantic to think of wine being made in dirty old barns or cellars, with primitive equipment by simple peasants, but so often such wines have dirty tastes, are vinegary, or turn cloudy in bottle after you have bought them. A press house or fermentation cellar should never be dirty.

R. S. DON: WINE.

"Steady on—hadn't you better start drinking a little sloe?"

Vitamin for Drive

It has been known for a long time that Vitamin B was an important growth factor for yeast. It is comparatively recently, however, that experiments done by myself and others have shown the great new potential opened up by using this vitamin regularly in every brew.

In a recent experiment I obtained 22% by volume (36 degrees proof) by direct fermentation. This brew, intended to be a dessert wine, was of course an attempt at perfection in alcohol production. It was based on grape concentrate and included all the additives recommended in this book. The Vitamin B cannot do the job on its own, but with a balanced must and suitable additives it does appear to achieve quite spectacular results.

I use a brand of Vitamin B1 called Benerva, obtainable through chemists. Tablets are obtainable cheaply, but do sell at various strengths from 3 mg to 300 mg. The maximum dose per gallon of must is about 15 mg, so you should obtain either 3 mg, 10 mg or 25 mg tablets (with the last named, a tablet can be easily split in two) . . .

In an emergency, with no tablets round, use a quarter of a teaspoonful of Marmite per gallon, which will assist matters considerably.

Bryan Acton: Recipes for Prizewinning Wines.

★　★　★

Clean Taste too

Cleanliness. Basically what is meant is that the wine should smell like wine, pure and unencumbered. Anything redolent of bad cabbages, old socks, vinegar, almond kernels, pear drops or any other clearly extraneous or foreign smells, should be regarded as suspect, to say the least.

J. M. Broadbent: Wine Tasting.

Campden Tablet

The proprietary name for a small tablet of potassium metabisulphite which when dissolved can release 50 parts per million of sulphur dioxide. Campden tablets are commonly added to must and wines to act as an inhibitor of micro-organisms and, in solution with acid used to rinse bottles, jars and all equipment before and after use. One to three Campden tablets are added per gallon of must according to the acidity, to inhibit the growth of moulds, bacteria and spoilage yeasts, until an active wine yeast can start the fermentation.

Many winemakers add one tablet per gallon of wine when racking to retard further yeast or bacterial growth.

B. C. A. Turner and E. A. Roycroft: AB-Z of Wine-Making.

★ ★ ★

... Unless

Like every beginner, I bottled too soon. When the corks popped, I took it for granted. I knew, as everybody did, that this was what you expected, and thought myself lucky that the corks had popped in a cupboard and not—like a bottle a friend was carrying—in a new car. Well, have you tried to sell a car with Australia, New Zealand and the New Hebrides outlined in wine stains on the light-coloured lining of the roof?

Duncan Gillespie: Lighthearted Winemaking.

Clobbered

Sodium metabisulphite . . . or its equally useful neighbour potassium metabisulphite, is available from all wine-makers suppliers and in most big chemists shops. I buy a pound at a time and dissolve it in a gallon of water, and use it again and again for rinsing out bottles, bins and other equipment.

It has a pungent smell, strong enough to make your eyes water and your nose run if you take a sniff at it, but any bugs damped with this ten per cent solution are "liquidated". As Saint Paul never said to the Corinthians "Don't scrap if you can help it, but if you have to clobber someone, clobber them good . . ."

On a smaller scale, you could dissolve two ounces of sodium metabisulphite or potassium metabisulphite in a pint of water, and keep it in a screwtop bottle.

DUNCAN GILLESPIE: LIGHTHEARTED WINEMAKING.

★ ★ ★

No Flying Corks

Anyone who has watched a jar of must bubbling through an airlock for a month will know better than to try to keep fermenting liquid in closed bottles. The use of fermentation locks, and racking, prevent the possibility of burst bottles. And wine should never be permanently bottled until the chance of renewed fermentation is negligible.

Forget all about flying corks and burst bottles. When proper methods are used, this can never happen.

JAMES MACGREGOR: WINE MAKING FOR ALL.

Bleaching

Unfortunately one cannot pour boiling water in one's glass fermenting jars or wine bottles but a good sterilising solution can be made up from strong household bleach (the stuff that "kills all known germs"). One pours 2 oz of this into a full size wine bottle and then makes up to one pint with water. Shake to mix then pour some into your fermenting jar or wine bottle, swill it around so that every inch of the inside comes into contact with the solution then tip it into your next jar or bottle.

A pint of this solution will sterilise a dozen fermenting jars or fifty wine bottles quite easily, but for heaven's sake don't forget to rinse the bottles out at least four times with cold tap water.

"UNCLE SID" IN A.W.

★ ★ ★

Magic and Sulphur

The Romans did at least know that cleanliness and fumigation were important in wine-making. Vats and vessels were washed out before the vintage either with sea water or with fresh water. Then they were scoured, carefully dried, and finally fumigated, sometimes with myrrh or else with myrtle, bay or rosemary. Before the vintage, too, when all is being made ready, "the wine cellar" says Columella "must be cleansed of all filth and fumigated with pleasant odours, that it may not smell at all mouldy or sour. Next sacrifices must be offered in the greatest piety and purity to Liber and Liberia and the vessels of the winepress . . ." One wonders if these preparations included a "magical" fumigation by sulphur; if so, the sacrifice would have been more efficacious.

W. YOUNGER: GODS, MEN AND WINE.

That Bug

Dirty equipment is probably the most obvious source of infection. Apart from providing sites upon which airborne bacteria may alight and proliferate, it will also attract insects, particularly the fruit fly Drosophila Melanogaster. Although these fruit flies (the so-called vinegar flies) are harmless in themselves, they frequently act as carriers of disease and can therefore spread infection from one place to another with amazing rapidity. Fermenting musts left exposed to the air, lees left in uncorked bottles or jars, splashes of wine from racking operations, and equipment of any description which has been put to one side still wet with wine, will attract fruit flies like a magnet attracts iron filings with the result that in a few days literally thousands of colonies of spoilage organisms may have developed from those small beginnings.

Cleaning-up should therefore never be neglected even though it is undoubtedly the most tedious chore in winemaking, otherwise much good wine may be lost by its becoming infected by bacteria or fungi originating from these sources.

Moreover, little effort is needed to clean and sterilise equipment soon after it has been used, whereas a day or two later a great deal of extra work will almost certainly be required, e.g., yeast allowed to dry on to the side of a glass jar is notoriously difficult to remove.

The prevention of infection and ease of cleaning are therefore two excellent reasons why dirty equipment should never be allowed to accumulate.

DUNCAN AND ACTON: PROGRESSIVE WINEMAKING.

★ ★ ★

"*What do you think of it dear? — my own recipe*"

Say When

It is an old French superstition not entirely without foundation that wine should be bottled when there is a clear sky and the wind is in the north. Furthermore, that wine should not be bottled when the vine is in flower. Possibly to most of us this is carrying the art a little too far; the day of bottling is likely to be governed by more mundane matters such as the maid's night out. FROM BARREL TO BOTTLE.

★ ★ ★

Best tip I ever got was to put all solids in a two-bob nylon mesh shopping bag and suspend in liquid portion of must. When it comes to straining off solids, this saves a lot of time, effort and mess, and of course the bagful can be used again for a second batch.

GORDON F. FORKES, PORT GLASGOW, IN A.W.

★ ★ ★

Off-Tastes

Most accidental off-tastes in wines are caused by carelessness on the part of the maker. Extraneous odours affect wines to a far greater extent than is generally realised, and wines may be spoiled by being stored in places where they come into contact with such strong-smelling things as petrol, insecticides, tobacco, or even scent.

LICHINE; ENCYCLOPAEDIA OF WINES AND SPIRITS.

*"I'm glad you find it agreeably dry and subtle
— it's my hair lotion"*

Thief

If you wish to taste wine in a large container there is
no need to buy a "wine thief" or to tip the container
up—just use an ordinary drinking straw and suck!

MRS. F. NICKALLS, EAST GRINSTEAD, SUSSEX, IN A.W.

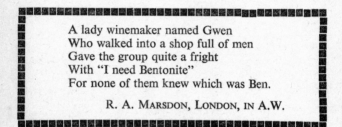

A lady winemaker named Gwen
Who walked into a shop full of men
Gave the group quite a fright
With "I need Bentonite"
For none of them knew which was Ben.

R. A. MARSDON, LONDON, IN A.W.

Give it Time

It can be said categorically that when home-made
wine disappoints, nine times out of ten the reason is
inefficient or inadequate maturing . . . within reason
the longer a wine is kept the better.

Since you are in effect fighting against yourself,
trying to keep the wine which you want to drink, a
system of making raids on the best wine difficult is
desirable. Put the wine you really want to keep at the
bottom of a stack and pile more ordinary wine on
top of it; or put the best wine in some other scarcely
accessible place. By making it harder to yield to
temptation, you automatically make it easier to
resist.

JAMES MACGREGOR: WINE MAKING FOR ALL.

CHAPTER FIVE

YEAST—
THE LITTLE
GREY CELLS

☼

Not Just a Squiggle

To so many winemakers yeast means a granulated substance bought in a packet, or a little squiggle on an agar-slope, or a brown tablet in a tube. But otherwise yeast, provided that it starts up a fermentation, remains very much a mystery that is best left alone: like a car engine, perhaps, or the inside of a television. You find a brand that seems pretty responsive for your purpose, and there you are; you buy it in the same way that you buy your petrol or your tea, and bother no more about it.

Probably at the back of this indifference is the minute size of a yeast cell. If this was the size of a dog, it might be difficult to get in the fermenting jar, but at least one could get to know it and recognise its distinctive differences from the ones used by our colleagues. As it is, twenty-five thousand need to stand side by side in a line to form an inch, so it is not surprising that they are known only by their retailers' names.

CEDRIC AUSTIN: THE WHYS AND WHEREFORES OF WINE-MAKING.

★ ★ ★

Best Heat

Wine yeasts are most active at a temperature between about 70°F and 80°F. At temperatures below 70°F fermentation becomes increasingly sluggish, until at about 40°F it sticks altogether; if the temperature of the vat rises above 90°F the yeasts become weak and fermentation stops. Fermentation at temperatures in the upper eighties is always dangerous, as other organisms detrimental to the wine, such as the vinegar bacteria, may become active before the alcoholic fermentation is complete.

R. S. DON: WINE.

"*Dissolves glass? . . . I'll have to write to Question
Time about this . . .*"

Why Wine Yeast

If bakers' yeast will produce a sound wine, why should one go to the trouble of buying more expensive wine yeasts?

This question, in various forms, is often asked by the novice in winemaking, who, seeing that he can buy an ounce of bakers' yeast for threepence or so, sees no reason why he should pay more.

The economics are indisputable, of course, for bakers' yeast is cheaper, though if one uses wine yeast from a starter bottle which is "topped up" with fruit juice, water and sugar after two-thirds of it has been used, the differential in cost diminishes rapidly in proportion to the length of time that the yeast is kept in use.

But, unless *all* you are concerned about is counting halfpence, cost is by no means the most important consideration; if you are in search of quality the use of a reliable, selected, sedimentary wine yeast becomes imperative.

Bakers' yeasts are cultured for their ability to produce a lot of gas quickly at relatively high temperatures, thus "raising" the loaf or other items being baked; they give a short, vigorous ferment. What is wanted in winemaking, however, is a slow, quiet ferment over a long period, at lower temperatures, and an ability to stand up to a high level of alcohol before succumbing, i.e., alcohol tolerance. These qualities are to be found in true wine yeasts.

Bakers' yeast does not always settle down firmly on the bottom of the fermentation jar, and the least disturbance or vibration will cause it to rise and cloud the wine, with a consequent wastage during racking (or siphoning). Wine yeasts will often give a really firm sediment, making racking appreciably easier.

If wine is left standing on bakers' yeast lees, it develops a definitely fusty odour, and consequently one has to be punctilious over racking; a wine yeast will allow you much more latitude in this respect and may even improve rather than spoil the flavour of the wine.

As you know, it is now possible to obtain wine yeasts of all types—Burgundy, Port, Champagne, Sauternes, Sherry, Madeira, Liebfraumilch—all sorts, prepared either as cultures, as powders, in liquid form, or as tablets. Do not be confused or worried by this, or be deceived into thinking that by using one of these yeasts you are going to produce a port, a sherry or a burgundy, and so on, from country wine ingredients. You will not.

You will, however, produce a fruit or grain wine with its full flavour unimpaired, and of the maximum strength, a wine which will be easy to rack and handle. And there may well be distinct differences of flavour between wines made from a single must, but fermented with different yeasts.

It is therefore great fun to experiment with different yeasts—if you wish—but basically the only "rule" you need to remember is that it would seem advisable to use a white wine yeast for a white wine, a red wine yeast for a red wine, and a Champagne yeast for a sparkling wine, i.e., to give a yeast sympathetic conditions in which to work.

To sum up, wine yeasts will give you:

    (a) More alcohol
    (b) Sounder wines, with no off flavours.
    (c) Firmer sediment, and thus easier racking, and
    (d) Subtle distinctions of flavour.

All in all, they're worth it!

C. J. J. BERRY, IN A.W.

★ ★ ★

Yeast, like every living creature (including home-brewers) needs sugar, proteins, mineral salts, and vitamins. Like home-brewers, yeast needs oxygen when reproducing; unlike home-brewers, it can live without oxygen the rest of the time.

SUCCESSFUL BREWING BY ROB ROY.

Choose the Strain

Many years ago the Grey Owl Laboratories marketed and still market a yeast of good, all round properties which was called All Purpose Yeast because it gives good flavour, is highly sedimentary, gives a firm sticky sediment, is a good clarifier, is unaffected by fluctuations in temperature and is able to produce high alcohol levels.

Nevertheless, such a yeast is *not* suitable for the production of Ports, Sherries, Madeira and Malaga or for the making of Champagne, neither will it produce the best flavour for specific kinds of wine such as Tokay, but it will produce good and well-flavoured table wines, both red and white, in the vast range of fruit and vegetable wines that amateurs so frequently like to make.

Consider the *properties* of various yeasts and in what way they are suitable for different kinds of wines:—

Champagne Yeast. This must be a heavy non-sticky yeast, sandy in nature so that it can be easily shaken down into the neck of the bottle. It must also be of good flavour as the yeast autolyses during the long process of Champagne production.

Burgundy, Claret, Pommard, All-purpose, Sauterne, are all sedimentary and for Red wine production only a Sedimentary yeast should be used as powder yeast such as port, etc., will remove a lot of colour from the wine. Sedimentary yeasts do not remove much pigment and wines made with them will have a good colour. Sauternes having a Sauternes flavour should not be used for red wines.

Port, Madeira, Marsala and Tokay belong to the class of yeasts known as powder yeast. These are small-celled, non-sticky, with a tendency to remain suspended in the wine, thus absorbing much pigment, rendering wine tawny after a time. They autolyse rather easily and in doing so confer their flavour on the wine, and should be used to produce wine of the particular type.

Sherry Yeasts. These are chosen for their ability to produce much acetaldehyde and to form a flor film under suitable conditions.

MRS. S. M. TRITTON IN A.W.

★ ★ ★

Surprises

Yeast is full of surprises. It is not always beneficial and can be a blight. For a layman like me it's a bit startling to learn that the microbiologists at Nutfield regard both dandruff and athlete's foot as yeasts.

Certainly the national collection's new catalogue of cultures which has just been published shows yeast strains from shrimps, bark beetles, Antarctic soil, and man.

There's even one listed which comes from the slime fluxes of *quercus kellogi*, and somehow my instinct tells me that it's not for home-made wine making.

In this respect Dr. Brown's recommendation is No. 177, a Californian grape yeast which, he says, has done his blackberry and apple wine a power of good.

JOURNALIST PHILIP CLARKE IN AN ARTICLE ON THE BRITISH NATIONAL COLLECTION OF YEAST CULTURES.

Necessity

However, if . . . dealers existed for nothing else, they would be useful simply as suppliers of wine and beer yeast. You could even make your own fermentation locks if you considered it worth while. But you could not make a good wine yeast.

JAMES MACGREGOR: WINE MAKING FOR ALL.

Yeast at Work

From his fermenting vats or tubs comes a tiny unforgettable and thrilling sound, the noise is unique and almost indescribable, but it is like the whispering of a thousand tiny leaves or the crinkling of ghostly tissue paper; it is the crushed grapes fermenting, and the sound is made by the bursting, on the surface, of countless little bubbles of carbon dioxide gas. At the same time, a pleasant, fresh smell fills the outhouse or fermenting room. The sound and smell of the "must" starting to work are things that the amateur wine-maker will always remember.

GEORGE ORDISH: WINE GROWING IN ENGLAND.

CHAPTER SIX

SO MUCH TO CHOOSE FROM

Winemakers' Market

Morning and evening
Maids heard the goblins cry:
"Come buy our orchard fruits,
Come buy, come buy:
Apples and quinces,
Lemons and oranges,
Plump unpecked cherries,
Melons and raspberries,
Bloom-down-cheeked peaches,
Swartheaded mulberries,
Wild free-born cranberries,
Crab-apples, dewberries,
Pine-apples, blackberries,
Apricots, strawberries;—
all ripe together
In summer weather;—
Morns that pass buy,
Fair eves that fly,
Come buy, come buy:
Our grapes fresh from the vine,
Pomegranates full and fine,
Dates and sharp bullaces,
Rare pears and greengages,
Damsons and bilberries,
Taste them and try:
Currants and gooseberries,
Bright-fire-like barberries,
Figs to fill your mouth,
Citrons from the South,
Sweet to tongue and sound to eye;
Come buy, come buy."

CHRISTINA ROSETTI "GOBLIN MARKET".

Wine Types

It is desirable, when making wine from various fruits to take some cognisance of the fact that some fruits lend themselves better to one type of wine than others. For instance, if it is desired to make a port type of wine, richly coloured red fruit like damsons, bilberries or elderberries are more suitable than, for instance, strawberries or light-coloured cherries. Fruits which have a very penetrating flavour, such as raspberries, should be used for a sweet wine and, as far as possible, the characteristic flavour of the fruit should be retained. Fruits which are very lacking in flavour, like white currants and pears, lend themselves better to a white table wine than would, for instance, the juice of a crab apple or a strongly flavoured dessert apple.

On the other hand, one can make use of apples for table wine production by reducing the flavour by the addition of syrup or choosing a cooking apple with very little characteristic flavour. Fruit wine making is more difficult because one can overdo the addition of syrup by not having tested the juice for its sugar concentration, but provided a little care is taken every bit as good wines can be made from English fruits as are made from grapes.

S. M. TRITTON: AMATEUR WINE MAKING.

★ ★ ★

Berry Dye

Not all black grapes provide a good colour in wine, and there is a tale that some vintners used to use elderberries to dye their wine. As a matter of fact there would be no harm in this; the elderberry makes an excellent wine by itself. But it would certainly not be allowed in the vineyards under the Appellation Controlée law.

EDWARD HYAMS. VIN.

Rhubarb Backbone

If you have a garden, the first and most obvious thing to grow is rhubarb. This is not because rhubarb wine is the best there is. On the contrary, rhubarb has practically no sugar, and a desirable step in making wine from it is to remove the oxalic acid which is largely responsible for the distinctive taste and colour of rhubarb. The resulting juice is thin and does not ferment well. But the most incompetent gardener can grow rhubarb by the stone, not the pound, and there is nothing easier to gather. Your rhubarb wine can be the backbone of your supplies; honest and unexciting if used on its own, but capable of much greater things if helped out by raisins, dates, lemons and oranges.

JAMES MACGREGOR: WINE MAKING FOR ALL.

★ ★ ★

Cool Drink

Gooseberry wine. "Its virtues—This is a curious cooling drink taken with great success in all hot diseases as fevers, smallpox, the hot fit of the ague; it stops laxation, stops bleeding; it wonderfully abates flushings and redness of the face after hard drinking or the like; provokes urine and is good against the stone; but those that are of a phlegmatic disposition should not use it".

PETER JONAS' "DISTILLERS GUIDE", QUOTED IN A.W.

"*That was clever, offering them some of your rhubarb*"

Composing

Of all the fruits in the world, the grape is supreme for
wine-making. It has (when at its best) the ideal
balance of sugar, acid, tannin and so on which can
produce a fine balanced wine. In Britain very few, if
any, of our fruits and none of our vegetables are as
balanced as the grape. However, by blending together
a number of ingredients into a composite fruit/
vegetable juice mixture we can arrive at a balance
which is in most cases as good as that possessed by
the grape. If you find that one of the ingredients is
not available, try to substitute for it a similar fruit or
vegetable, and in this way you will ensure that the
balance is maintained.

BRYAN ACTON AND PETER DUNCAN: MAKING WINES
LIKE THOSE YOU BUY.

★　★　★

Rich Tint

Elderberry wine. The elderberry is well adapted for
the production of wine. Its juice contains a con-
siderable portion of the principle necessary for
vigorous fermentation, and its beautiful colour
communicates a rich tint to the wine made from it.
It is, however, deficient in sweetness, and therefore
demands an addition of sugar. It is one of the very
best of the genuine old English wines, and a cup of it
mulled, just previous to retiring to bed on a winter's
night, is a thing to be "run for" as Cobbett would
say; it is not, however, agreeable to every taste.

MRS. ISABELLA BEETON (1891).

Banana Skins

From Edinburgh, Walter J. Gunkel writes: Some banana recipes require the skins to be included in the "boil-up". This causes the liquor to turn an unpleasant black/greyish colour. What is so important about the skins? Can they be omitted and a substitute additive used which would preserve the banana colour of the liquid?

Wine made from bananas only are entirely different in flavour to those which include some of the skins. If we are making a straight banana wine, then it has been our practice to omit the skins and add a cupful of white grape concentrate. This retains the pale golden colour of the wine.

The procedure is different if you are wanting to add body to, say, an elderberry wine, which is strong in flavour. Then boil up the skins as well to obtain any sugar which may be present.

We have found that banana wine clears quickly, and when bananas are used in any wine, it clears far more quickly than wines which do not include them. Why? We don't know, but it has always worked!

QUESTION AND ANSWER IN A.W.

★ ★ ★

Too Much Fruit

Dr. Beech went on to say that at Long Ashton they had come to the conclusion that generally in wine-making too large quantities of fruit were being used. They had found that excellent wine—not necessarily tasting of the original fruit—could be made with as little as 1 lb. of fruit per gallon of water, plus 2 lb. of sugar, yeast, and nutrient, etc. If one crushed apples in the presence of 150 parts per million sulphur dioxide and extracted the juice one got a perfectly white wine with an intensely vinous smell.

REPORT IN A.W.

Vinosity

There is one other very important aspect of blending ingredients . . . It has been pointed out on numerous occasions that certain amateur wines, chiefly those based primarily on ingredients other than fruits, lack a nebulous "something" in their character.

This rather nebulous feature has been termed vinous quality or vinosity and is really a broad appreciation of a wine as a wine as opposed to an alcoholic beverage.

Unfortunately it is almost impossible to give a more precise description since any attempt to do so would be more likely to confuse than to clarify the issue.

The winemaker may nevertheless rest assured that the palate will at once find a wine lacking vinous quality to be deficient in some respect even though the reasons for coming to this conclusion may not be immediately apparent.

This serious fault can easily be prevented by including raisins, or better still, grape concentrate in the must, about 1 to 2 lb. of raisins or $\frac{1}{2}$ to 1 pint of grape concentrate per gallon usually being adequate for this purpose. Indeed the routine use of grape concentrate as a standard ingredient for every must has much to commend it since wine quality is sure to benefit from this practice.

The extra expense incurred in this way is partly off-set by a corresponding saving in sugar (1 pint of grape concentrate replaces 1 lb. of sugar). In addition, the cheaper brands of grape concentrate are perfectly satisfactory for improving the vinous quality of a wine so that its cost will only be increased by a few shillings per gallon even when 1 pint of grape concentrate per gallon is employed.

PETER DUNCAN AND BRYAN ACTON: PROGRESSIVE WINEMAKING.

Aroma of Rasp

Raspberry. A delicious soft fruit, which is easily prepared by liquidising and steeping or fermentation for one or two days on the "pulp" producing a wine generally with the unmistakable aroma and flavour of the fruit. Loganberries are very similar in composition and style and both are eminently suitable for table dessert wines in particular. Due to the high flavour and acidity care needs to be taken not to exceed the quantity of fruit required. Test the acidity and flavour dilution with a small quantity of fruit before making up a gallon "must" of the style required.

J. R. MITCHELL: SCIENTIFIC WINEMAKING MADE EASY.

★ ★ ★

No Stripping

As both keen winemaker and keen amateur field botanist, I am alarmed to read recipes recommending the use of large quantities of wild flower heads in flower wines. As most people will know already, many common wild flowers are becoming rare because they are picked in such quantities. Could I therefor appeal to readers not to strip a bank of its primroses or cowslips or even its humble dandelions, for if they do, there will soon be none left for other people to enjoy . . .

Life is difficult enough for wild flowers nowadays, without winemakers helping to exterminate them.

MRS. A. KLENZ, CHELMSFORD, ESSEX, IN A.W.

Too Late

There were blackberries in the hedge—gleaming black and shiny—but we country people didn't pick them after October the 10th because after that date they say "the Devil's piddled on them".

M. HARRIS: ANOTHER KIND OF MAGIC.

★ ★ ★

Elderflower

Wine from the elderflowers can be made as a sparkling champagne comparable with the French limonade aux simaux, or as a still, light table wine with its own special perfume and flavour. The flowers should be picked when dry on a sunny June day with the tree at the height of its blossom and perfume. The very best wine is made from fully-open florets shaken from their stalks straight into the collecting basket. Two-thirds of a pint measure of florets, not pressed down, is more than enough for a gallon of wine.

NEVILLE WEAVER IN A.W.

★ ★ ★

Birch Rhenish

In March the ends of the birch boughs are cut off, and bottles are suspended from them. To every gallon of liquor add 1 lb sugar. Yeast is added and fermented: mace and cinnamon added. Said to be "a most delicate, brisk wine, of a flavour like unto Rhenish".

E. SPENCER: THE FLOWING BOWL.

Best for Mead

In our view the finest meads are made from single-blossom honeys and of these, clover, acacia, orange, rose, wild-rose and rosemary are outstanding.

They are easily obtained from most stores these days, though if one can obtain English clover honey direct from a bee-keeper it is worth the slight extra expense. The reason is, of course, that such honey is fresh and, in common with other winemaking ingredients, will produce better mead because none of its delicacy has been lost during storage.

Mixed blossom honeys rank next as mead-makers, but the mead does not have quite the same character and its flavour will generally prove poorer than that obtained from single-blossom honey.

Below these honeys we place heather (or ling) honey . . . It is entirely a matter of the time element. If you are a patient winemaker and can wait eight years, then put heather honey up near the top of your list, but not otherwise.

Most of the honey sold in shops does not fall into any of the categories just mentioned. It is labelled "Blended" and often in small type, one can see that other things have been added to the honey so that it will spread better on bread and so on. These blended honeys are really of little use for making mead since the product will lack character. Such honeys, however, are useful when making melomels and metheglins if cost is important, since the honey plays a lesser part in these drinks.

There are some excellent Australian honeys, both single-blossom and blended, but one needs to guard against the admittedly rare chance of purchasing eucalyptus blossom honey, which has a peculiar but typically bitter flavour. Most Australian honeys, it should be emphasised, are entirely satisfactory. So, too, is New Zealand honey, indeed in most respects it is very similar to our own native honey.

Honey from such countries as Mexico, Jamaica, Guatemala, and Rumania often have an advantage in that they are less pure than honey from Britain, Canada or the U.S.A. The eternal quest for purer and purer honey is not in our view a symbol of advancement but rather the opposite. One sometimes overhears beekeepers commenting on the problem of pollen clogging their filters when purifying it. They seem blind to the fact that it is many of these so-called "impurities" in honey which give it its bouquet and flavour.

BRYAN ACTON AND PETER DUNCAN: MAKING MEAD.

★ ★ ★

Nectar

The only fermentation process which may go back beyond Neolithic times, and which may be even older than agriculture, was the turning of honey into nectar. Rock paintings, found in Southern Spain, show honey-collecting in an Early Stone Age hunting community. When farming began, one of the associated industries was bee-keeping.

LORD RITCHIE CALDER: THE INHERITORS.

CHAPTER SEVEN

GRAPES—THE ULTIMATE

They Ripen Here

Grapes produce the ultimate in wine, and contrary to the popular and widespread public belief in this country are easily grown and regularly ripened out of doors in most areas of Great Britain. Disbelief of this arose from failures when would-be growers were sold varieties of vines that were cold or hothouse cultivars by ignorant and misleading nurserymen. Such varieties will never succeed without the protection, heat and lengthened season afforded by a glass-house. This iniquitous practice is still in operation, most comprehensive plant catalogues still recommend indoor varieties for outdoor use, and on radio programmes the "experts" stubbornly adhere to similar recommendations. It is not until we can educate those so-called authorities that belief in the success of viticulture in this country can be established.

GILLIAN PEARKES: GROWING GRAPES IN BRITAIN.

★ ★ ★

The Vine, I am sorry to say
Has a very discouraging way
Of presenting its yield
To the birds of the field,
The blackbird, the thrush and the jay.

H. HEATH, WESTON-SUPER-MARE.

All-Weather Work

Growing English wine we expect to make a reasonable living, but we do not expect to grow stinking rich. The work is hard, the hours are long and it has to be done in all weathers. Time, tide and the grape wait for no man.

The risks are always there from the time the vines break bud until the wine is bottled and sold. So why on earth do we do it? Well, of course, there *is* a certain romance about it all. It is, after all, the *second* oldest profession on earth, but the romance can wear a little thin after spending a day pruning vines in a blizzard or sinking posts in a heatwave.

Personally, I love wine and I love working in the open air, and I can think of nothing on earth so satisfying as growing fine wine; to wrest from a soil as heavy as ours a wine which has a flowery fragrance and spicy fruitfulness is an end well worth achieving.

W. B. N. POULTER OF CRANMORE VINEYARD, ISLE OF WIGHT, IN A.W.

★ ★ ★

Holiday Guide

The grape-vine, while it will tolerate winters of great harshness with temperatures as low as—20°F, needs the warm, wet spring weather which creates a green and pleasant land, enough rain in early summer to keep it so, and unbroken fine weather during the late summer and the early autumn to bring the grapes to that perfection which depends upon warmth and sunshine.

Thus a prospective holiday-maker planning his holiday could do much worse than begin by asking himself—where do wine grapes flourish?

EDWARD HYAMS: VIN.

Britain, English Vineyard Wine

Hambleton 1970/71. Estate-bottled Sir Guy
Salisbury-Jones. It is very easy to mistake Sir
Guy's excellent wine for a dry Vouvray or a crisp
Moselle. The vineyard slopes south on the Hamp-
shire downs, north of Portsmouth. Bot. £1.15.

ENTRY IN "WINE MINE", SUMMER 1972.

★ ★ ★

Hard Under-Foot

Treading looks easy. Lyrically one might consider it
to be merely a stroll among grapes. It is not so. When
you get into a *lager* your first shock is one of cold-
ness. You expect the grapes to hold the warmth of
sunshine that has ripened them out on the hill. But
they are as cold as pebbles on a river bed. You expect
also that they will crush easily, that they will be
merely frail skins of tissue around the pulp. But
under the naked foot they are agile, evasive and
resistant, trying to avoid their approaching change
into alcohol. Only gradually does the juice spurt
between the toes. And when you stand with the bare
backs of your knees against the granite walls of the
lager, cold stone against your legs and cold grapes
under your feet, and when you look at the tumbled
sea of fruit that you must crush—10,000 lb. of
grapes—the labour seems Herculean and the naked
foot too frail.

W. YOUNGER: GODS, MEN AND WINE.

*"I promise dear — I promise, I'll never sneak any
of your wine grapes again"*

Iechyd Da

Fine Rhineland grapes like the Muller Thurgau,
French like the Seyve Villard and the British Wrotham
Pinot have already been cropped from four acres of
experimental vineyards, carrying 8,800 plants, in
Carmarthen, Pembroke and Cardigan. . . . Experts
in viticulture think there is a big future for wine-
growing in west Wales.

Said Mr. Gwilym Jones, horticultural officer for
Carmarthen: "We are stockmen here, not crop
growers, and it may take years to acquire the know-
how of vine growing. But we are learning fast."

A Welsh Wine Growers' Association has been set
up to advise on techniques, and help producers with
labelling and marketing and—when the time
comes—the payment of excise duties.

FARMERS WEEKLY.

★ ★ ★

British Wine

What the amateur does in a plastic dustbin in the
kitchen is being done scientifically by several firms in
Britain, chief among them Vine Products, part of the
Showerings offshoot of the giant Allied Breweries,
who produce over six million gallons of British wine
each year . . . The raw material of British wine is
grape concentrate imported from varying sources:
Cyprus, Greece, South Africa, Spain, even South
America. If the climate and soil around Kingston
were of the right type for growing grapes, Vine
Products would need a giant vineyard extending as
far south as Epsom, as far west as Weybridge, and
covering thirty square miles to provide enough
grapes for their present output.

THE BEVERAGE REPORT.

CHAPTER EIGHT

SERVICE, PLEASE

☼

Elegance

A lot has been written about the right type of glass to use for different styles of wine, and this is where, to a certain extent, art takes precedence over science, but both factors have to receive consideration.

The initial, almost sub-conscious, appraisal of a wine is the way in which it is served—the colour of the wine, the salver and glasses all contributing to the general sense of pleasure. It is obvious that a brightly ornamented salver will spoil the general appearance of the offering and similarly coloured or decorated glasses will detract from the appreciation of the wine's colour. For this reason, clear glass is superior but who can deny the enjoyment of taking a cut glass of wine from a silver salver? The cut crystal, whilst having a pattern which perhaps prevents a clear sight of the wine, at the same time adds an elegance which enhances the moment of appraisal.

J. R. MITCHELL: SCIENTIFIC WINEMAKING MADE EASY.

★ ★ ★

Perfection

The perfectionist washes his glasses with unscented soap, rinses them in clear water, dries them with a non-fluffy cloth, polishes them with tissue paper, and puts them away bowls upright—precautions aimed at ensuring they acquire no smell.

Lacking perfection, it is wise before serving fine wine to smell the odd glass because washing machines can leave deposits of detergent at the bottom of the bowl.

If a rinse with spent tea leaves fails to remove wine stain from decanters, use a bleach solution. Then rinse thoroughly with cold water and do not use decanter again for several days until no smell of bleach is present. ADVICE IN "WINE MINE".

Don't Let Fly

It may seem a slight to the reader's intelligence to explain how to open a bottle of sparkling wine but, like most things, there is a right and a wrong way.

To add an air of gaiety to a celebration it is common practice to let the cork or stopper "fly" and the wine gush out. At the risk of being spoil-sports, this is the wrong way to open sparkling wine. A released cork with somewhere in the region of 50 p.s.i. behind it can be dangerous should it strike anyone in the face (this occurred at the National Wine Festival in 1971 when a steward was hit in the mouth by a stopper which flew immediately the wire was removed).

So always cover the stopper with a napkin, holding it on tight, and pointing away from you and the guests, as you untwist or cut the wire hood.

Then allow the pressure to push against your hand, as you ease the stopper gently out.

Should the wine be very lively the napkin will also prevent the wine gushing out over everybody before you can get it into the glasses. Never try to control a gushing wine by putting your thumb or the palm of your hand over it, unless of course you don't mind getting an eyeful.

J. Restall and D. Hebbs: How to Make Wines with a Sparkle.

★ ★ ★

Different

The climate as well as the food has to be considered. For example, a charming light wine with a highly refreshing acidity drunk with fresh trout on the banks of the Loire in midsummer or a vinho verde enjoyed with rich pork in the Minho can taste entirely different on a cold and misty autumn evening with "smokies" in Arbroath. The colder the climate, the more full-bodied the wine needs to be.

J. M. Broadbent: Wine Tasting.

✳ ✳ ✳ ✳ ✳ ✳ ✳ ✳ ✳ ✳ ✳ ✳

The bottle screw whose worth, whose use
All men confess that love the juice:
Forgotten sleeps the man to whom
We owe the invention, in his tomb.
No publick honours grace his name,
No pious bard records his fame.

ODE TO THE CORKSCREW, WRITTEN IN 1732.

✳ ✳ ✳ ✳ ✳ ✳ ✳ ✳ ✳ ✳ ✳ ✳

★ ★ ★

Patience

It is not elaborate precautions that are needed to see
that a wine is at its best when you drink it (and is it
not wasted if it is not at its best?) but a little gentle-
ness and a little patience. If you realise that the wine
has been cooped up in its bottle for five or perhaps
ten years when suddenly, at the drop of a hat, you ask
it to put on its best performance without warning,
you can see that it may easily be a bit shy. And shy,
despite the mockery that usually follows the use of
words like this about wine, is just what it very often
is. You open it, you drink it, and just as you are
swallowing the last drop of what has been (at the
price) a frankly disappointing bottle you suddenly
get a whiff of magic; the scent has begun to come
out, the wine has begun to expand and show itself,
like a peacock spreading its tail. But it is too late.
You have finished the bottle.

HUGH JOHNSON: WINE.

74

Aroma

It sometimes comes as a surprise to learn that the mouth can detect only four basic tastes: sweetness, saltiness, acidity or sourness, and bitterness, every other component of a flavour being detected as an aroma. . . . While there are only four basic tastes, there are literally thousands of aromas and millions of olfactory glands capable of distinguishing between them. These receptors are embedded in a mucous membrane in an upper chamber of the nasal passage. Aroma is detected only when the substance responsible flows over this sensitive area. It cannot be detected if air is not inspired, even though the nose is filled with the aroma that diffuses continually into the olfactory region.

As with taste there is also adaption to aroma. Gentle inspirations cause a steady response: if the aroma is breathed in more deeply the initial response is greater, but this falls off quickly with successive inspirations.

With deep inspirations the aroma is rapidly lost. Anyone who has breathed deeply into a bunch of violets will know that the aroma seems to fade, and that the nose has to be brought nearer and nearer to the flowers to capture the aroma . . .

Adaptation is only temporary and is broken after the original aroma has been removed for a short time.

BEECH AND POLLARD: WINEMAKING AND BREWING.

★   ★   ★

Experienced Glance

"A sight of the label is worth fifty years' experience" —a cynical truism; for what an impressionable lot we are! Even the most sternly disciplined taster is biased by the merest glimpse of the label, even by the shape of the bottle.   J. M. BROADBENT: WINE TASTING.

Detection

Then at the party, came this glass of wine.

"What do you think of that?" the lady asked, with an artless smile. I tasted the wine, swilled it round my mouth, swallowed, and breathed in through my nose. A sunburst of flavours assaulted my taste-buds simultaneously, some of them pleasant and some less pleasant, and I realised that I *knew*.

"It's a bramble wine, about four years old" I said.

"Easy, as it happens. The slightly tawny colour shows that it has matured for a year or two. The very distinct taste of tannin betrays the fact that it is bramble wine, and not a wine made from some of the other berries like raspberries. As a matter of fact, it has been fermented on the pulp a shade too long; I keep the time down to four or five days, but this has been kept on the pulp for ten days or a fortnight with the result that it is a little harsh. But a bramble wine, without a doubt . . ."

Saying nothing, the lady brought the bottle over to me. The label showed that it was in fact a blended red wine, probably a mid-Mediterranean blend of Rhone and Algerian wines, with a name like Marche-commune Grandplonque Rouge Reserve . . .

Sometimes in bed at night I summon up to the palate of my memory that sunburst of flavours. It still tells me "This is bramble wine . . ." but I should have kept my mouth shut and swanned around the subject until I saw the label.

DUNCAN GILLESPIE IN A.W.

CHAPTER NINE

THE TRUE AND PROPER DRINK

☼

The Ballad of Boozledon

I am a happy booze runner, with a production line,
I've set the town of Boozeldon awash with beer and
    wine,
For years I have been brewing, it always was tax free,
Though it wasn't really legal 'til the year of '63.

We brew it in a dustbin, and drink it by the pail
You name it and we'll make it, lager, stout or ale.
If our stocks are running low, somebody will shout
"Let's have a drop of heavy in, and lay these fellows
    out."

We are all good noshers too, just every kind of dish
Steak and chips, or Goulash, or even Flying Fish,
Pies of Cheese and Bacon, or a bowl of Cook-up
    Rice,
Roll mops and Heimishers, all are very nice.

A cheerful band of drinkers, together we all stand
Maybe a bit unsteady, with tankards in the hand.
'Prentices or Craft Brothers, we have our little joke,
We are always drinking, but the Publicans go broke!

KEN SHALES: BREWING BETTER BEERS.

★　★　★

Thirst Quencher

There is nothing in the world that can quench an
honest English thirst like honest English beer; when
the load of hard, dirty repetitive work begins to
weigh heavily on the shoulders, beer will strike new
heart into a man and spur him on to fresh efforts.

BOB COPPER: A SONG FOR EVERY SEASON.

Good ale, the true and proper drink of Englishmen. He is not deserving of the name of Englishman who speaketh against ale.

GEORGE BORROW.

* * *

Change

To show Englishmen, forty years ago, that it was good for them to brew beer in their houses, would have been as impertinent as to gravely insist that they ought to endeavour not to lose their breath; for in those times, to have a house and not to brew was a rare thing indeed. Mr. Ellman, an old man and a large farmer in Sussex, has recently given in evidence before the House of Commons, this fact: That forty years ago there was not a labourer in his parish that did not brew his own beer; and that now there is not one that does it, except by chance that the malt be given to him.

WILLIAM COBBETT IN 1821.

* * *

The Kofyar make, drink, talk and think about beer.

AMERICAN ANTHROPOLOGIST.

Suit Yourself

Beer making can be all things to all men (and women too). If you are allergic to mess, you adopt a technique which may involve a little more trouble, a little more time, and possibly more expense, but which will be as clinically unmessy as anyone could wish. If time and trouble are the principal things you can't afford, there are methods of making beer with so little effort that by far the most arduous and time-consuming stage in the whole operation is the stage of drinking the beer. If you don't want to become an expert, there's no real need. You follow one of the simplest methods blindly, rigidly, every time, and your beer always turns out exactly the same.

JAMES MACGREGOR: BEER MAKING FOR ALL.

★   ★   ★

Simple Start

It's not a bad idea to start off on them (kits) so as to get familiar with the basic handling of brews without too many complications or distractions. The occasional brewer, too, might make them more or less a permanency. The thing is that they amount to "foods of convenience" and it is obvious that they are rather more expensive than buying the ingredients separately and doing the assembly in the kitchen.

Many home brewers use 200 or more gallons of beer in their household every year, without riotous consequences at that, and on this scale a few pence per gallon begin to show up. At present this can be done from basic ingredients for less than a pound sterling per week, hardly an excessive drink bill when one considers that it is less than two hours pay for a craftsman in the motor industry.

KEN SHALES: ADVANCED HOME BREWING.

Do Not Make Your Beer Too Strong

At first sight this may appear to be extraordinary advice. "Surely the whole point of brewing my own beer" you may well ask "is that by so doing I can have a better beer than I can buy?" And "better" for most people, is at first synonymous with "stronger".

But strength is even less the principal criterion of a good beer than it is of a good wine.

After all, the extra strength is easy enough to achieve; one has merely to use more malt or sugar, and ferment for a longer period, and it is quite feasible to produce a beer of, say, wine strength, up to 10%-14% alcohol by volume.

But is it desirable? Breweries will tell you that their strongest beers are by no means the most popular, and the answer does not lie simply in the fact that they are more expensive.

The most popular beer in Britain is the weakest—mild.

Why is this? Surely the answer lies in the beer drinker's approach to his drinking. The beer drinker, unlike the wine lover, expects to be able to drink a fair quantity, say three or four pints, without ill effect; it should make him pleasantly relaxed, but not make him drunk, or leave him with a splitting headache the following day.

Any beer drinker who has had an "evening out" drinking a high gravity (i.e., strong, quality) beer will know what I mean!

That is why your habitual beer drinker prefers the lower gravity bitters and milds; he can drink them for a whole evening's darts without risk.

Surely the same is true of home brewed beer? It is neither wise nor hospitable to brew beer so strong that after two glasses your friend slips under the table or has a severe headache next day; he will not thank you for it! Home brewed beers are not a whit inferior to commercial ones but they are often made far too strong, with disastrous results upon host or guest, and it is this which earns them a quite undeserved bad reputation.

Therefor aim at making your brews of roughly the same strength as the principal commercial types you are emulating and do not fall into the error of making them so *very* much too strong. If you *must* produce double-strength beer or "barley wine", then please, please, treat it with respect, warn your friends of its strength and serve it in smaller glasses, as publicans do their "nips" and "specials" and NOT in pint glasses or tankards.

YOU HAVE BEEN WARNED!

C. J. J. BERRY: HOME BREWED BEERS AND STOUTS.

★ ★ ★

No Royal Road

. . . the object of home brewing is to get the beer the way you want it. No real craftsman is ever satisfied with his work, and seeks always to improve it. There is no royal road to success in home brewing. Reading helps, especially if you have enough scientific background to study professional works on brewing. Even books intended more for the general reader can often provide background knowledge, which is exceedingly helpful . . . It is all rather like a jigsaw puzzle, when the key piece turns up, the whole picture rapidly comes together. Clean systematic working, using measures, hydrometer and thermometer are essential. So is the keeping of records. Don't just make a change or worse still several changes at once, without keeping records. It would be galling to produce the beer of a lifetime, and be unable to reproduce it.

KEN SHALES: BREWING BETTER BEERS.

"*Do you have to wear that ridiculous outfit when you make mead?*"

Our Methods Too Complicated ?

As a fully trained brewer, I am no longer practising in the industry and to provide myself with the cheap beer which I used to get free, I have been forced to brew my own.

A friend of mine gave me several back numbers of your excellent magazine and while I cannot with authority quibble with the articles on winemaking I am bound to say that some contributors' statements on home brewing are wide of the mark.

... Another fallacy concerns the age of hops; brewers have known for a long time that as far as bittering is concerned the age and aroma of hops is not very significant, and although in commercial practice I never did so, I have brewed perfectly palatable beer from hops that were so old that some of them had mould growth on them.

I could go on at length, but I do feel that more people would brew at home if only the process appeared a little more simple. I have in my time tried a number of fairly complicated grists but the results (though very good, in my own estimation anyway) did not justify the extra work, so I have cut out all solid grists in favour of extracts and this is what I recommend:

8 lbs DMS	4 oz hops
2 oz brewers yeast	6 fluid oz of finings
4 oz of sugar.	

The above grist can be a little improved by a teaspoonful of Irish moss but it is not essential, though I always use it myself.

The procedure is as follows: dissolve the DMS malt extract in three gallons of hot water. Pour into a boiling pan or, if available, a Baby Burco wash boiler, add the hops, and, if you wish, the Irish moss, and bring to the boil; continue boiling for an hour.

Pour off hops and wort mixture through a quarter-inch plastic mesh in the bottom of a colander. Pour the wort back through the hops to make sure all the "break" is filtered out and whilst still hot place the wort in your fermenting vessel. (N.B. make sure that if it is a plastic one it is of the high density type which will not contaminate the beverage).

Sparge the hops to remove all the residual wort, using water of as high a temperature as is possible. Add your spargings to the contents of the fermenting vessel and make up to five gallons with hot water.

Allow the wort to cool: by adding it to your fermenting vessel hot, you will have ensured sterility.

Take some of the wort into a clean container, cream up the yeast and when working add to the worts which should be at a temperature of 70° F. for choice but below 80° F.

Allow to ferment: depending upon temperature this will take from two to four days. The original gravity being in the region of 10/50 and a finishing gravity of 10/10 being aimed at.

Take a sample, make sure that it is reasonably clear and not a thick opaque appearance that fully fermenting wort has and rack off half a gallon into a clean jar.

I never bottle my beer, it is too much trouble, but rack it into a cask to which I have added the finings and four ounces of sugar; I then top up with part of the contents of the half gallon jar and seal the container.

After a day the beer is ready to drink although of course it will be slightly "green" still: I allow the first runnings to emerge under the pressure generated by the yeast working on the sugar primings. I do not worry about clarity too soon, it is bound to be fairly cloudy but if drunk in a tankard one doesn't worry about this too much; subsequent drawings can be drunk from a glass and will be crystal clear.

I only spile the cask when or if the pressure drops sufficiently to make it necessary and before drawing off beer insert a tube with a wad of cotton wool in it so that air being drawn into the cask is filtered; note no ju-ju palaver over a fermentation trap is needed.

In this way if you want to keep your beer for some time you will find that if you do it correctly it will last for at least three weeks.

I believe you will agree that the above cuts out a lot of mumbo-jumbo which all amateurs in any field of activity are prone to.

One final word despite many experiments with proprietory yeast cultures I have yet to find one that is really satisfactory; always use *Brewers'* Yeast obtained from a brewery and unless you have the necessary equipment and time never try to collect your yeast for further use. And note I have made no mention of skimming either to remove hop scum of yeast; it simply is not necessary.

R. J. N. BOOTH'S ARTICLE IN A.W. SPARKED OFF MUCH DISCUSSION AMONG HOME BREWERS, TO WHOM SOME OF THE ADVICE BY A PROFESSIONAL WAS HERESY.

★ ⟨★ ★

Cheap Hops

Naturally, good hops are not cheap, but I can honestly state that "cheap" hops can be very expensive in the long run. Imagine making a high quality barley wine, maturing in bulk and bottle for months, and finding out, after all that, that the beer is deficient in flavour or has deteriorated due to the poor preservative value of the bad hops used. Like the grape, the hop has different varieties, and the yield and quality varies with the soil and climatic conditions. . . . The two main hop growing areas in the U.K. are Kent and Worcestershire, and neighbouring counties. Good hops are grown in both areas, but the aristocrat is reckoned to be the East Kent Golding, which gives the aroma and clean taste to our best pale ales and bitters, which are the height of English brewing skill.

KEN SHALES: ADVANCED HOME BREWING.

Know Your Malts

Pale malts are easily obtained and it is possible to get three different grades, all of which are fully modified grains, but differ in the period of time they have been left in the kiln.

Lager malt is our first, and is only lightly cured so that very little colour is imparted to the finished beer.

Pale malt, the second in this group, is used mainly for making bitter beers and some stouts.

Mild malt is number three, and, as its name implies, is used for mild ales and stouts. This malt is roasted the longest out of the three pale malts and of the trio is the most expensive to make though the amateur usually is charged the same rate for each of them.

All pale malt contains active enzymes that are only waiting for the correct conditions to set them to work again, so completing the conversion to maltose and dextrines. In other words, all malts that are labelled Pale malt, Lager malt, Mild malt, need to be mashed and they are the main ingredient of all beers. It is possible to buy those ready crushed for mashing at a little extra cost.

Amber malt is on the market now and is very useful to the brewer, for it is possible to make just that little difference to your brews by its addition. It is roasted in a cylinder and, again, still retains some diastatic action so needs to be included in the mash.

Brown malt, on the other hand, contains no diastatic activity, for the enzymes have been destroyed in the higher temperature used in the roasting. This is a good grain to use in brown ales, and needs only to be boiled to extract its colour and flavour.

Black malt (Chocolate or Patent) sold under all three headings, this malt is fully roasted until black in colour. Once again all enzymes have been destroyed by the high roasting period, so this only needs to be boiled to extract its colour and flavour so characteristic in stouts.

Crystal malt is possibly the best known of all to the amateur. It is called a green malt, for after the germination period it isn't dried in the usual manner before roasting but placed in the revolving roasting cylinders at a temperature of 150° F. - 170° F. The grain being full of moisture, a form of mashing takes place, converting the starches to maltose which then crystallises. This again is a useful grain to add in small quantities to give your beer a little individuality. It is easy to use, for it only needs to be boiled.

Wheat malt is much more difficult to process as the grains have no protective husk as is the case of barley. It is used mainly to give a little extra body to beers and is mashed along with the other malt grains.

Malt extract is made from lightly cured barley that is mashed around 130° F.: it is boiled under vacuum at about the same temperature to produce a diastatic syrup or powder. Most manufacturers make three grades of syrup, marketed under their own brand names, plain, high diastase, and one with added caramel.

The powdered extract is in two grades, plain and with caramel added.

High diastase malt extract will convert large amounts of unmalted cereals in the mash tun. If you do not intend doing this there is no need to pay the higher price that it usually commands. Used in a mash with grain or on its own, malt extract should always be boiled in the wort.

Concentrated Brewers' Worts which contain hops as well as malt syrup, do not usually need boiling as this has already been done for you. There are still a few more malt products, but they are not generally available to the amateur brewer.

As a quick and easy guide you could say that Pale malts are the basis of all beers and need to be fully converted in a mash tun, whilst the darker malt grains are used for adjusting flavour and colour, and need not be mashed.   ERIC CLARKE IN A.W.

A.W., 1/72, pp. 32-33.

Tang Goes

In my experience, all malt extracts give the best results if they are boiled with hops or hop extracts. The so-called "malt extract tang" quoted against home brews on this basis, arises almost entirely from neglect of this process. If one visits a malt extract factory, the air is full of this smell and taste, which can be recognised in the beers made without boiling.

KEN SHALES: ADVANCED HOME BREWING.

★ ★ ★

Hop Perfume

Hop oil preparations are attracting interest at the moment. These vary in price, and your supplier will indicate approximately the requisite dosage. These are the essential oil of hops (of the nature of a perfume) and not the oil of hop seeds (of the nature of linseed or sunflower oil).

A pure essential oil of hops would be used at the rate of one drop per barrel of 36 gallons, so mostly they are diluted to give ease of usage.

Take about a quart of the beer, and incorporate the hop oil with vigorous stirring. Then rouse into the main bulk. The best time for the operation is when the beer is primed. Used intelligently, they are beneficial in raising the aroma. If one just drops them in and hopes for the best, it's a waste of time and money, but that goes for most things in this game. As the German proverb has it "Malt and Hops are wasted on a fool".   KEN SHALES IN A.W.

A.W., 3/70, p. 157.

89

Hops and Sex

Sensitive readers may skip this paragraph. In the English hop-gardens, sex rears its head. Not among the pickers (or at least, not only among the pickers). Male hops are allowed to grow here and there among the female hops, and when the time comes, the golden pollen is carried by the wind to the female flowers. English hops contain seeds, Continental hops do not—in the great hop-growing areas of the Continent the female hops are grown in seclusion from the males, and the result is that no seeds form. This is just one of the differences between the two.

SUCCESSFUL BREWING BY ROB ROY.

★ ★ ★

Try Honey

Honey is an unusual ingredient for beers, though country folk have added it at times. However, many Boozewrights will buy honey by the drum for addition to wines, making mead, etc., and it is then economical to use it in beer formulations. I prefer a mild pale single blossom Australian honey such as "Salvation Jane" or "White Clover" obtained from Rogers (Mead) Ltd. This is technically suitable and not expensive. It can replace sugar in lager formulations, especially if a fine Continental hop variety is being used, and can also fit into strong dark lagers. The aroma is superb . . .

In fact, an experimentally minded brewer can develop a whole new dimension in brewing with honey. Devotees of Health Foods who object to refined sugar will be happy with this information.

KEN SHALES: ADVANCED HOME BREWING.

"Oh, hello dear . . . er . . . um . . . I found this
body in one of my best vats"

Body from Bran

The only adjunct I use is the best and most trouble-free I have found—ordinary bran. This gives a fine "malty" flavour, contains enough gluten to guarantee a superb "body" and luscious head to the brew, yet, as it is low in starch, there is no hazing difficulty. When it is used, the beer clears quite normally.

I use it at 3 to 6 oz, to the gallon, according to the "body" required—3 oz for light ales and lagers, 6 oz for heavy stouts, etc. The bran is simmered very gently with the extract and grain malts for 45 minutes, then the hops are added and given the same time longer, a few extra hops being added in the last five minutes.

H. Huckstep in A.W.

> There was a young vintner called Hewer
> Who fancied himself as a brewer,
> The smell from his flat
> Killed a whacking great rat
> That had spent all its life in a sewer.
>
> R. Bicketon, Coatbridge, in A.W.

Breakfast Beer

Shredded wheat, one biscuit per gallon, is good in mild ales. The strongly flavoured cornflakes can be used, but their taste persists in the finished beer, and causes raised eyebrows. Still, it might be a breakfast beer, and cheaper than milk at that!

Ken Shales in A.W.

Keep Moving

By the way, the day will come when an evening's
bottling is quashed because of outside circumstances.
Don't despair, and don't let the brew stand idle.
Add 4 oz sugar in syrup to your brew and it will
ferment on happily for another 24 hours. Ignore it,
and off flavours can develop and your brew may even
be spoilt. A "spoonful of sugar" can save the day.

DEAN JONES: HOME BREWING SIMPLIFIED.

★   ★   ★

Best Friend

Maturing. This is a most important phase in beermaking and the fact that it comes right at the end of
the whole process does not lessen the importance;
good beer can be spoiled by bad maturation.

Naturally bottled beer, that is beer bottled with
some yeast still in it, depends upon maturation to
obtain the fullness of flavour that we enjoy so much.
A well-matured beer usually retains its head long after
being poured, whereas a beer that is inadequately
matured will quickly lose its head. A good guide on
how long to mature a beer is to take the starting
gravity, deduct 20, and mature the beer for one month
for every remaining 10 degrees. This may seem quite
a long time, but experience has proved its worth . . .

It may be that certain home-brewers will question
the value of this longer period of maturation that we
advocate. Before the war of 1939-1945, when natural
beers were the order of the day, the major breweries
never sent out their beers before they were five to six
weeks old. If the professionals felt that this wait was
worthwhile, then amateurs, such as ourselves, can
surely afford to wait. Time is our best friend.

B. C. A. TURNER AND D. J. MOON: SIMPLE GUIDE TO
HOME-MADE BEER.

American Guide

One of the main causes for flat beer is the American tendency to serve it too cold. The ideal temperature is 45° F. for beer and 50° F. for ale, although it is customary to chill as low as 40° F. for lager and 45° F. for ale. Do not chill below 40° F., and the nearer the beer is to 45° F. the better it will taste. Imported beers should be served at 48° F. to 50° F. and English ale or Irish stout should be served at 55° F.

GROSSMAN'S GUIDE.

A certain fermenting fanatic
Spent his days making beer in the attic:
He tried a new brew
With his wife's Irish stew—
And produced a result quite dramatic.

MR. AND MRS. D. RHODES, GRANTHAM, LINCS.

Open Throat . . .

And then I knew how good beer could be. Of course, the fault had been in myself; I had tried to drink beer the way one should drink wine; by sipping it. And there are few things in this life so revolting as sipped beer. But let it go down your throat "as suds go down the sink" and you will quickly realise that this is a true friend, to be admitted to your most secret counsels. Long draughts with an open throat are the secret.

MAURICE HEALEY: STAY ME WITH FLAGONS.

Spoiled by Lime

Nobody seems to be sure why lager has suddenly come into such popular favour, the trend being much more marked than can be accounted for by such contributory factors as the rise in the number of women beer drinkers. Great efforts are made by the brewers to get just the right delicate flavour which so many people seek to remove by adding lime juice to the drink. ("Mind you" remarks one brewer philosophically "they can rub it in their hair for all I care, so long as they buy the stuff").

D. SUTHERLAND: RAISE YOUR GLASSES.

★ ★ ★

Five gallons of brew take little more effort than one gallon, and last nearly twice as long.

NOW TRADITIONAL SAYING.

★ ★ ★

Say Where

Now, where to ferment your brew? I am fortunate in that I have a cellar. Remember, fermenting beer does make a smell, nectar to a lot of us but not so to others. I am told that clothes do not improve with the smell of beer so that rules out the airing cupboard. So the "where" to ferment is important if there is to be harmony in the household. I have converted a large ply packing case (to hold a ten gallon carboy plus several gallon jars) for brewing beer and fermenting wine. It is insulated and has a small heater and thermostat.

DEAN JONES: HOME BREWING SIMPLIFIED.

Dean Jones: Home Brewing Simplified, p. 15.

. . . But Not Too Open

The habits of record pint-swallowers have so worried Guinness officials that they may drop all such feats from their Book of Records.

There may be no more after next year (1971). The Board of Guinness Superlatives, who produce the book, will make a decision later this year.

An official said: "Some of the records have got to such extremes that it is dangerous to try to break them."

He said someone was injured recently while trying to break the record for drinking beer while standing on his head.

"Whenever anyone telephones us now with a query about one of these records we always mention that medically it is extremely inadvisable to try to break them."

Guinness chiefs also feel that the activities of people who drink up to 65 pints in an hour are bad for the company image.

The drink chosen for recent attempts has been draught Guinness.

STORY IN "LICENSED TRADE NEWS".

CHAPTER TEN

COMIC...

�֍

There was an old fellow called Batey
Whose wine-making problems were weighty,
When he'd had a few glasses
He'd an eye for the lasses—
But the problem was Batey was eighty!

R. N. WHITE IN A.W.

★ ★ ★

Mixed Sticks

Boozeldon Police were called to the premises of the Thirst National Bank in Bitter Street in the early hours of yesterday morning, where they found that the premises had been entered. Attached to the safe was a bundle of dried bananas and a detonator.

Fingerprints found on the premises belonged to one W. (Bill) Sykes, a local top screwsman and peter expert. As the police were surrounding his residence there was a terrific explosion and floods of sticky red liquid were scattered all over the area.

Mr. Sykes was pulled from the ruins alive but badly shaken. The sticky red liquid, on analysis, proved to contain bilberries, raisins, and traces of plastic explosive.

Mr. Sykes told our reporter "When I come out, I'll be more careful with my labels".

KEN SHALES IN A.W.

Giddaduvit!

. . . I contracted the dreaded Du-Lally Tap, an occupational hazard of Vintners and Amateur Oenologists.

Briefly, this disease is caused through active yeast cells entering the pores of the skin. Drinking fermenting must is another source of infection, causing a quivering action all over the body, due to the fermenting yeast, under the skin, attacking the sugars in the blood stream.

The symptoms are at first giddiness and later as the ferment proceeds and the yeast is producing alcohol faster than the body can consume it, drunkenness.

If this condition is suspected it can be confirmed by placing a fermentation lock in each ear-hole and the degree of "plopping" will indicate how far advanced is the disease. The only cure is to drink enough sugar solution (using say 14 lb sugar) to enable the yeast to produce sufficient alcohol to kill itself.

A sherry type yeast produces a further condition of Saxatile Compactum, this gives a profusion of bright yellow flowers, except that on reaching out for them, they elude one's grasp.

A Lager or Bottom Yeast gives an invert condition, causing the toes to turn under, eventually biting into the sole of the foot. By using simple but special deduction methods and by bitter experience I have evolved a simple but effective cure which I would be happy to pass on to any fellow-sufferer.

In the process I have acquired much out-of-the-way knowledge which has enabled me to produce some fantastic wines, especially when I used the paraffin drum by mistake instead of the barrel.

ROSE HIPS, NOT ENTIRELY SERIOUSLY, IN A.W.

Spoof Letter

The Vicarage

From: The Rev. John McHaig, LL.D., B.Sc.

Dear Friend.

Perhaps you have heard of me and my nationwide campaign in the cause of Temperance.

Each year for the past fifteen years, I have made a tour of England, and delivered a series of lectures upon the evils of drinking.

On these tours, I have been accompanied by my assistant, Reginald Fortescue. Reginald was a pathetic case, a young man of good family and excellent background, whose life had been ruined because of excessive indulgence in beer, whisky, rum, gin and other strong drink.

Reginald would appear with me at lectures and sit on the platform, drooling at the mouth and staring at the audience with bleary and bloodshot eyes, whilst I would point him out as an example of what drinking would do.

Unfortunately, last winter Reginald died.

A mutual friend has given me your name, and I wonder if you would care to accompany me on my next tour and take poor Reginald's place.

Yours very sincerely,

John McHaig

J. McH/VWS

Spoof letter which crops up periodically.

★ ★ ★

Inn-Spectre!

The Guild's New Year party was in full swing and wine flowed freely, when the "bar" was visited by a ghost. "Sorry: We don't serve spirits" was Fred's only unruffled remark. E. A. ROYCROFT IN A.W.

Snake Test

I have been reading the comments on the use of meat in making wine. I am interested in a particular aspect of this. I remember the World War II stories of saki and how the Japanese would put a live snake in it. The amount of time the snake remained alive was supposed to indicate how good (or strong) the drink would be . . .

If the object of the snake was to supply protein for yeast food my calculations say that if you use more than one ounce of snake per gallon you are wasting snake. ROBERT J. SMITH, DAYTON, OHIO, IN A.W.

★ ★ ★

Warning

When a bottle of stout was opened for the purpose of satisfying curious friends, its dark-coloured gassy contents escaped rather hurriedly and leaked through the floorboards of the boxroom, thus giving our lounge ceiling a most unusual pattern of brown-upon-white in one corner. The airing cupboard walls are most attractively splashed with the contents of a bottle of yeast "starter" which exploded; even the wall in the spare bedroom had its wallpaper dampened when a bottle of gooseberry champagne, which was being stored on one wall, blew its cork, which in turn shot across the bed to the other side, taking with it precious liquid.

The paper on the chimney breast was stained a gorgeous pale pink when a gallon of beetroot wine (which was again being kept in the warmest place) bubbled through the air lock and dripped fermenting beetroot all over the fireplace. It did look rather suspicious when a policeman friend called in soon afterwards!

BARBARA THORNE SAYS "BEGINNERS BE WARNED"
IN A.W.

Ferrari Fiasco

After all, if you want to spend your evenings boiling up sloes, bananas and raisins to make "Chianti" no one is going to stop you, but many British wine-makers must have been amused to find that what in this country is a small-scale hobby had become in Italy a mass-swindle. In 1968 the Italian police made a mass arrest of over 200 people who had flooded the country with fifty million bottles of fraudulent "wine". You may have drunk some of it yourself; the brew was sold all over Italy and exported to Britain and Germany. So massive was the fraud that experts reckoned that in one year a third of all Italian wine was faked. The materials used to make the wine (which bore such respected names as Nebbiolo, Barbera, Valpolicella, Soave, Bardolini, Asti and Lambrusco) included figs, dates, dried apples, synthetic alcohol, molasses, beans used for feeding mules, and artificial colouring made from the scum dredged from the bottom of banana boats.

D. COOPER: BEVERAGE REPORT.

★   ★   ★

The Ferraris . . . were boosting their wine with an extensive advertising campaign. This included posters depicting an ecstatic mountaineer sampling the Ferrari product and exclaiming "My, what a wine!" There was also a popular television "commercial" in which a tired business man was depicted coming home to his family after a heavy day at the office, out of sorts, grumpy and of no use to anyone. But his wife had the answer. She gave him a glass of Ferrari wine. The effect was magical. "Look I'm a new man!" cries the husband, prancing like a two-year-old.

. . . The wines taste good, and, even under normal analysis, appear genuine".

ALAN MCELWAIN, REPORTING TO THE SUNDAY TIMES FROM ROME.

And Later

Rarely have Italian police been so embarrassed. From practically under their noses, exhibit A in the Great Wine Case was spirited away. Exhibit A took quite a bit of stealing. It is 2.76 million gallons of allegedly adulterated wine produced by 270 accused wine-makers in one of Italy's biggest mass trials.

The wine, police say, would have filled 300 tank trucks. Yet it was not only syphoned off with, apparently, the greatest of ease from four carefully sealed cellars in Ascoli Piceno, in Northern Italy, where the trial is being held, but the thieves lingered long enough to replace it with equal amounts of coloured water.

. . . The trial was adjourned again, pending the recovery of Exhibit A—if ever.

ALAN MCELWAIN, FROM ROME.

★   ★   ★

Home-Bruin

Prohibition in America produced "home-brewers" of which the American papers of the time said—

Woman says that after her husband drinks home-made hooch he becomes as wild as a bear. Another case of home-bruin.—*New York Morning Telegraph.*

"Egypt had home-brew four thousand years ago" observes a contemporary. No wonder they knew how to pickle their mummies so well.—*Columbia Record.*

"Punish the home brewers" urges a zealous citizen. Does he think they aren't being punished? —*Kansas City Star.*

And an awful warning against distilling at home—

The best way to cure snake-bite with bootleg whisky is to let the snake drink it before he bites you. —*Nashville Tennessean.*

Please Ignore Jack's Hints Please!

Jack Dixon's tongue-in-cheek accounts of wine-making are eminently quotable, and it is only by an effort that the selection is kept down to large slabs from three articles, "Winemaking made (qu)easy", "Simple Cellarcraft" and "Circle of Squares".

The object of this article is to shatter some of the taboos which abound in our craft, to tear away at least a part of the veil of mystery and ritual which have been set up over the years by superstitious winemakers, and laid down as laws to be followed blindly.

To begin, you need not buy a lot of expensive equipment, so resist the advertisements and look round your own house for suitable containers. I often ferment 20 gallon batches in the bath. Not very clean, you think? Well, modern deodorants can easily keep you smelling sweet till bottling time.

Smaller batches can be managed nicely in old chamber pots. I had a chamber pot of carrot wine maturing very well under the bed in the spare room. It would have been a winner had the wife's mother not come to stay over Christmas. Some people just don't *think* before they act.

Sterilising is another obstacle set in our path. Please don't scurry round the chemists asking for obscure chemicals with unpronounceable names. Household bleach cleans toilets and false teeth very efficiently, so it must be good for our purpose and is very cheap and easy to obtain. Perhaps your finished wine will taste and smell slightly of chlorine, but at least it is a clean smell which may well earn you extra points for bouquet in competitions.

Ingredients are another subject on which one is given a great deal of misleading information. Many authors warn about certain things not being suitable

*"Well well — I often wondered where this bottle of
sulphuric acid got to"*

because, I suspect, they like to keep their best recipes to themselves:

Recently I opened a batch of privet leaf wine. My grandfather was so thrilled with it that no-one else had a chance to taste it. He didn't even leave us a bottle to open at his funeral last week and his last words as he died were: "Oh! That privet leaf wine!" High praise indeed!

Another fallacy I would like to expose is the one about using only the rind and juice of oranges. Go ahead and use the pith, if you wish: it gives a unique flavour which a discerning judge will appreciate. One bottle of my own orange wine was in a competition not long ago, and I heard the judge remark to the steward: "What's he put in this? My God, it tastes like pith". At least, I *think* that was the comment. It didn't win a prize, but was returned with a label attached bearing the words "Highly Condemned" which just goes to show that one does not have to be able to spell to judge wines.

Simple unscientific methods are easy to follow and remember. To test acidity, for instance, I drop a dirty new penny in the must; if it is bright and clean in one hour that means too much acid; if it is not clean in 48 hours, I add more. About 12 to 24 hours means the acidity is just about right.

Fermenting is another subject needing only a little applied logic to enable you to dispense with thermometers. Yeast is a living thing, no-one will deny me that. Well, so is the human body, and if you place your finger in the must for one minute, the colour of the finger shows if the yeast can live. Blue—too cold. Red—too hot. Simple, isn't it?

You will find that in time the use of my methods will alter your wines beyond your wildest dreams. Your friends will shudder in anticipation when you offer your wine.

When you enter your clubroom people will nudge each other and a respectful silence will fall on the room.

These things and more have happened to me. At

the last meeting but one, some of our committee members were even urging me to leave our small circle so that I could give other circles the benefit of my experience. It is all very touching, and I don't like the idea of leaving them, but if they lock me out just once more I shall take their advice.

I might even join *your* Circle, if you are very lucky.

Fourteen months later, in the A.W., Jack Dixon took extracts from Wakeford Wine Circle Newsletter!

Our last meeting, held in the village hall (said the mythical newsletter) consisted of a talk entitled "Brewing Stronger Beers", by a gentleman named Cecil Barry, or something like that, from somewhere down south—Endover, I think it was. He was a very nice fellow, and probably would have given a very good talk if it had not been for his sudden illness. He was in quite good health before the meeting began, drank a pint of old Granny Wood's Treacle Ale, and even asked for the recipe.

But when Mr. Barry started speaking he had this funny turn, so we pushed him the five miles to the station in a wheelbarrow and put him on the train in the guards van with one of Farmer Briggs' best milking pails; we hope he sends the pail back when he feels better.

The monthly competition, judged by Mr. Finney, the plumber, was for the best flower wine, sweet. It was won by our postmistress, Mrs. Dovey; Mrs. Clarke, the vicar's wife, was second, with Squire Poole a very close third. The scuffle between the judge and Farmer Briggs' wife had nothing to do with the order of judging, but started when Mr. Finney gave his comment on Mrs. Briggs' cowslip wine. "It smelled just like cowslip" was the comment. We think she must have misheard him.

So much for the meeting, now for the general news. The vicar has poured away five gallons of his 1968 plum wine. He was doing a bit of experimenting with that batch. He said it was a great success, but when his wife tried a glass he could not keep her from chasing the choirboys. We asked for the recipe, but he says he will carry it to his grave. Pity!

Our postman, Mr. Bottomley, bought some fancy chemical, Rohamlet B, for softening fruit, when he was in town. Last week he tried some in the water when bathing his feet. It took out two corns, softened his ingrowing toenail, and rotted the turnups off his trousers.

The midwife, Mrs. Brown, borrowed a few bottles of bilberry port from Mrs. Dovey; she finds that two glasses while assisting at a birth help her to put up with the moaning and groaning.

The village squire, Mr. Poole, has finally solved his problem. If you remember he made five gallons of dry sherry which developed a most unusual bouquet in the stone jar. On bottling he found a long cigar butt amid the sediment. It goes to show: even rich folk can have troubles.

Jack Dixon also had good advice to offer on "Simple Cellarcraft"—

Finished wine is not always to your taste. Adjustment can be made, but should not be undertaken lightly. Logic is the thing to use.

Over acidity is a common fault, especially in light table wines. Despaireth not! The remedy is to be found in most households. One level teaspoon of stomach powder or one crushed indigestion tablet stirred in a gallon of wine, is just as effective in neutralising acid in wine as it is in your stomach. Excessive CO_2 is removed in the same operation, a satisfied burp will be heard bubbling up through the air lock. With the heavy bodied wines this noise can be most embarrassing, so make sure the cellar door is firmly closed.

The lighter wines can be converted into Champagne type by a very simple process. . . . Rack the wine into champagne bottles and have the corks

"*I propose Nellie Dean*"!

and wires handy. Now drop one "Alka Seltzer" tablet in each bottle and cork quickly. This sparkling wine can be consumed as soon as the tablet has dissolved, no sticking it down in a cave for two years, or growing long thumbnails for dégorgement.

Another fault, not quite so common, is "mousey" wine. So-called experts will tell you to pour it down the sink. This is very wasteful because it can be cured. It is simple when studied logically. Pour in a "catty" wine. A slight vinegar taint does not need hiding, blend it with a nice, crisp potato wine to bring out a delightful flavour.

When checking a wine with a pH paper, I inadvertently dropped cigarette ash on to the wet paper, which promptly turned green. So now to cure over acidity I empty the ashtry (no, not the dog ends, Madam, just the ash) into the wine.

It can now be disclosed that I have been asked to give a serious talk to the largest, most advanced circle in our district.

Their offer has been accepted, of course, but I am worried by their stipulation that I redden my nose and wear baggy pants, and put on a funny hat. Even more puzzling is the fact that I must deliver this serious talk on their party night.

Ah well! Such is fame! JACK DIXON IN A.W.

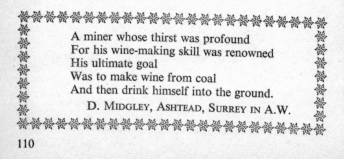

A miner whose thirst was profound
For his wine-making skill was renowned
His ultimate goal
Was to make wine from coal
And then drink himself into the ground.

D. MIDGLEY, ASHTEAD, SURREY IN A.W.

CHAPTER ELEVEN

CURIOUS...

☼

Sherry Mice

There was one thing, however, which I had not expected to see, of which I had never read. I had not expected to see at floor level by one of the casks a grill work to which were attached pieces of dry toast. These, I was informed, were for the mice. Mice were encouraged and cats kept off the premises. I saw a number of mice who were appreciating the care which had been taken for their safety and their comfort. They were extremely small. It seemed to me that it would be very easy for them to push aside the light covering of the bungholes. I remembered being told years ago that at one time rabbits were put into Sherry casks, that the alcohol in the wine fed on them and was enriched. I wondered, watching those midget mice, but I decided it was more prudent not to be inquisitive.

ALEC WAUGH: IN PRAISE OF WINE.

★ ★ ★

"The Samagorean wine was so strong that more than forty men were made drunk with a pint and a half of it, after it had been mixed with water". ARISTOTLE.

★ ★ ★

Seeing Pink Men?

Three elephants smashed their way out of the Kruger National Park and wandered around in a drunken spree, flattening the farm crops. They had to be shot. What intrigues me is that the Game Rangers said that the animals had apparently eaten over-ripe maroela tree berries which fermented in their insides making them drunk. Are these strongly fermenting berries used for wine, I wonder?

A. E. ROYCROFT IN A.W.

Mush!

Ethyl alcohol—a poison taken internally by human beings for thousands of years. A substance so simple to make that it often makes itself. Ripe fruit lying in a watery mush at the base of a tree quickly ferments and forms alcohol. I have often seen elephants which have been feeding underneath one of these trees go charging off like runaway bulldozers, cutting great wavy paths through the bush. And warthogs, so drunk they could not hold their tails up, stagger off bumping blindly into every anthill. Early man got his first hangover in the same way, but it did not stop him from coming back for more. OMNIVORE.

★ ★ ★

Drastic Method

I made some Peach wine and bottled it. It was of sufficient quality to pass the eagle palates of the Harrow crowd. I left it in my office overnight and during the night the building burnt down. Typewriters and adding machines were melted into grotesque heaps of metal and plastic. The glass panes had shattered and fired themselves in thousands of needle splinters into the hardboard screen. Only two things survived. One was a bottle of wine, badly blackened, and the other was a badly charred but still usable corkscrew. As I gazed at the chaos, I remembered Dale Carnegie's axiom. "When you only have a lemon, make a lemonade".

So we opened the bottle, and found that it had become a sort of instant Madeira, quite pleasant to drink. I am not sure what sort of temperature is required to make Madeira in about one hour (that was the time of the fire) or whether the hoses of the seventeen fire brigades were instrumental, but you can always try it yourself! BRYAN ACTON IN A.W.

That All?

Sent by Mr. R. Dean, 3 Pinelands Way, Osbaldwick, York—After a recent Wine Circle meeting a friend of mine came out of the club and made towards his car; he fumbled about in his pockets until he eventually found his car keys. The door seemed difficult and hard to find before he managed to open the door, but eventually he fell into his car.

He was about to attempt to start it when a policeman who had been watching him for the last few minutes, walked over to him, took out his notebook and pencil, and started to ask him questions.

After he had written his notes and departed I went over to my friend and asked him rather apprehensively what the policeman had wanted.

"Oh" he replied "He only wanted the recipe for my parsnip wine!"

QUOTED IN A.W.

★ ★ ★

Kvass—a refreshing Russian beer home-brewed from rye, barley and malt, and flavoured with mint or cranberries.

LICHINE: ENCYCLOPAEDIA OF WINES AND SPIRITS.

★ ★ ★

Earliest of Us?

Cranberry wine deposited in a birch-bark pail in the bronze-age oak coffin buried in the Danish Guldhøj . . .

J. G. D. CLARK: PREHISTORIC EUROPE.

Potent Pulp

In Europe, *Agave Americana* can be found naturalised in the Mediterranean regions, in particular along the Costa del Sol seaboard of Southern Spain, where it forms impenetrable hedges, and fringes the roadside verges.

This Mexican native is used to make an intoxicating liquor known as pulque, by fermenting the sap exuded by the flowering stem when cut. Pulque was of such a potent nature that King Netzahualcoqatl forbade its sales to any but the feeble and aged, nursing mothers, and soldiers on the march.

In Mexico there are still stringent rules regarding the manufacture of this drink, though the death penalty is no longer the reward of bootleggers, as was once the case.

I do not believe that pulque is made in Spain: perhaps the low price of alcohol has removed the stimulus that causes wine making clubs to thrive in Britain.

A. M. GARROD, CASTLE DOUGLAS, IN A LETTER TO THE "GARDENER'S CHRONICLE".

★ ★ ★

"They can squeeze Bordeaux out of a sloe and draw Champagne from an apple".

ADDISON. TATLER 1709.

★ ★ ★

Keep Level on Yoghourt

Scientists investigating the effect of alcohol on motorists have established that a 10 oz carton of yoghourt consumed before a drinking session reduces peak blood alcohol levels by 67 per cent, that is to say by about the same as a normal meal.

NEWS STORY.

Home Brew in Utopia

Wines we have of grapes, and drinks of other juice, of fruits, of grains and of roots; and of mixtures with honey, sugar, manna, and fruits dried and decocted; also of the tears and woundings of trees; and of the pulp of canes. And these drinks are of several ages, some to the age or last of forty years. We have drinks also brewed with several herbs, and roots, and spices; yea with several fleshes and white-meats, whereof some of the drinks are such, that they are in effect meat and drink both; so that diverse, especially in age, do desire to live with them, with little or no meat or bread. And above all we strive to have drink of extreme thin parts, to insinuate into the body, and yet without all biting, sharpness or fretting, inasmuch as some of them, put upon the back of your hand, will, with a little stay, pass through to the palm, and yet taste mild to the mouth. FRANCIS BACON: NEW ATLANTIS 1627.

(Spelling modernised).

★　★　★

Keeps Going

As far as ageing is concerned Tokay is a slow starter. The extreme sweetness makes fermentation a long and slow business. It continues to ferment sporadically in cask, but particularly in the spring (when they used to say it started to work in sympathy with the sap rising in the vines from which it came) when the warm weather affects the cellar-temperature and humidity. In the famous wine-merchant's house of Fukier in Warsaw, which even in this century had Tokay of the vintage of 1606, followed by dozens of vintages of the seventeenth and eighteenth centuries, they found that very old wine, even after years in bottle, used to ferment again very slightly in the spring. HUGH JOHNSON: WINE.

116

"I see you have all the usual brews!"

Black Wash

Another—to me—startling fact that the Guinness people came up with is that some Chinese in South East Asia wash newly-born babies in Guinness.

How the practice came about is still a mystery, but one theory is that it is connected with the tradition in the same area of washing babies in black honey wine. Guinness looks similar to the wine, and is probably cheaper. JAMES MURPHY IN "REVEILLE".

$$\star \quad \star \quad \star$$

Famous Case

In one famous case a reputable wine merchant, in a large University town, sold elderberry wine under various labels and made a handsome profit. Imitations of port, claret and burgundy wines made from elderberry were sold in vast quantities to dons and undergraduates who eulogised its vintages knowledgeably. A number of people in the business suspected the outrage because they knew how little real wine was being imported and could see the outstanding amount being sold, but there was no proof, and no certainty. Eventually this happy merchant retired a rich man and only on his death-bed did he tell his son the truth. Most of the famous wines he had sold had been made with elderberry, then adapted, flavoured and coloured with brown sugar and vinegar to suit the bottle and label.

ANDRE LAUNAY: EAT, DRINK AND BE SORRY.

Ladies, it is uncomely to drink so large a draught of wine that your breath is almost gone and you are forced to blow strongly to recover yourself: throwing down your liquor as into a funnel is an action better for a Juggler than a gentlewoman.

ACCOMPLISHED LADY'S RICH CLOSET OF RARITIES,
1753.

You can eat it too

Brewers yeast is available in many forms and can be taken in tablets or added to food. There is a variety that tastes like cheese in flake form; another variety has been smoked over hickory, and has thereby a pleasant bacon flavour that is palatable in appropriate recipes. An ounce of brewer's yeast daily is recommended.

FREDERICKS AND BAILEY: FOOD FACTS AND FALLACIES.

* * *

A wine for slaves, from a recipe by Cato—Grape pulp 10 parts, boiled grape juice 2 parts, vinegar 2 parts, fresh water 50 parts, old sea water 64 parts. Mature for 15 days.

QUOTED IN "MAN MAY DRINK" BY RICHARD SERJEANT.

* * *

A number of scientists agree that alcohol from fermented fruit juices might well have been the first painkiller.

M. B. KREIG: GREEN MEDICINE.

CHAPTER TWELVE

...AND CONTROVERSIAL

✿

Embalmed . . .

When the metabisulphite has been added, all natural yeasts are at once killed, and with them the natural bouquet, and possibly a great many other elements of whose existence we are not yet aware. Vegetable matter so treated is not only dead, it is embalmed, and will keep for ever, like the Egyptian mummies.

MARY AYLETT: COUNTRY WINES.

★ ★ ★

As somebody has said, wine is like sex; nobody will admit to not knowing all about it.

HUGH JOHNSON: WINE.

★ ★ ★

. . . Barmy ?

Such recent developments as the use of the hydrometer, sulphite and wine yeasts, unheard of when most recipes were compiled, simply had no place in traditional books of this type. Indeed, some authors even went so far as to militate violently (and often incorrectly) against the introduction of any modern innovations. Although it need hardly be said that this attitude is outmoded and prejudiced, traditional ideas do die hard and still, unfortunately, have many adherents who are content to follow recipes and old practices blindly without giving any thought to what they are doing. How consistently high quality wines can be expected under these circumstances is a matter for conjecture!

DUNCAN AND ACTON: PROGRESSIVE WINEMAKING.

Courtesy

If the fruit from which a wine has been made is not the grape, the appellation "wine" is only a courtesy title. The thirst for alcohol, which appears to be deeply rooted in the human race, is so strong that if grape-wine is not available, other fruits are turned to account. Europe, especially in those parts which fall just outside the wine-belt, such as Poland, northern Germany, and much of Russia, fruit wines are made in very large quantities.

... In remembering some of the nauseating brews one has drunk (and praised) among the country wines, one is apt to forget the few, the very few, of quite promising delicacy which have been encountered.   L. W. MARRISON: WINES AND SPIRITS.

★   ★   ★

Fizzy Bridge

In the United States, Lancers, which is described as crackling, and in Britain Mateus are the biggest selling wines of all. They are, in a sense, wines for people who do not really like wine. They form an intermediate stage between childish fizzy drinks and the adult taste for wine. As such, they do an invaluable service, for anything that leads more people to drink wine as part of their daily diet helps them towards health and happiness.

HUGH JOHNSON: WINE.

A L'eau There?

I wonder: do wine snobs ever realise how foolish they are and what untruths they tell? Malcolm Moyer, of the 400-year-old Ruddy Duck, has been laughing at them for some time. As a trap for wine snobs he inserted in the restaurant's wine list "L'eau Duponde" (otherwise pond water) describing it as "matured locally. A heady wine, varying in colour. It should be drunk with a pinch of salt." The demand for it was tremendous and over fifty real snobs were caught in three months; such as the young man who told his friend it was a wonderful vintage which he had previously had in London.

Now that he has proved his point, Mr. Moyer of the Ruddy Duck, near the village of Peakirk, considers the joke over. He has put up a notice "Owing to increased local demand, my supplies of L'eau Duponde have dried up and I do not anticipate any further supplies."

"WINEMAKER'S LOG" IN A.W.

★   ★   ★

No Compliment

The producers of Champagne do not accept the story that Louis XV, enamoured both by Champagne and Madame de Pompadour, had the glasses for one moulded of the bosom of the other. They say instead it must have been an enemy of Champagne that designed them as they ensure that the wine, once poured, goes flat and warm as quickly as possible. They advocate the flute or tulip glass for champagne and add the smaller the bead (bubble) in the wine the better the quality.   E. A. ROYCROFT IN A.W.

Poor Granny's Image

"Sparkling Syrup of Figs" was how Ian Howie described his first efforts at wine-making in a PoW camp in Czechoslovakia during the war. He churned out a mixture from old raisins and prunes distilled in clandestine vats made from old lampshades—and couldn't keep up with demand.

Now he is faced with similar demand for the rather more palatable stuff from his Merrydown winery at Horam, Surrey, which 20 years ago was a derelict 17th century mansion on a five-acre bed of nettles.

. . . Merrydown's reputation grew phenomenally with the aid of a newspaper that in all seriousness printed a leg-pull of Howie's—"After two or three glasses they start setting about the landlord".

. . . More lines were introduced, all sounding like something that granny rushed up in a mad moment—redcurrant, rhubarb, gooseberry, bilberry, and so on. And the idea arising from the association—that either the stuff poleaxes you after one glass or acts as an instant laxative—dies hard indeed.

But although most of those who taste are converted, Howie long ago gave up trying to beat the granny image in the London hotels. "Though you can get a glass of chilled gooseberry wine (not unlike a good Moselle) in the Sydney Hilton, just try getting one in Park Lane" he commented. "We merely infiltrate from beneath".

PRUFROCK, SUNDAY TIMES, INTERVIEWS IAN HOWIE, JOINT PARTNER IN MERRYDOWN.

★ ★ ★

The breath test is unquestionably the greatest single life-saver yet discovered.

RICHARD MARSH, MINISTER OF TRANSPORT 1968.

Richard Marsh, Minister of Transport, commenting on the results of the first year of the breathalyser, December 1968.

Rubbish?

Why do amateur winemakers bother with rubbish? Dandelion, Goats-Beard, Kohl Rabi, Cowslip and similar un-wine like ingredients should be left to the insects. Certainly wine, of a type, may be made from virtually anything, but let's get the hobby in perspective.

Tasty, sound, reliable, clean wholesome fruit and syrups are there for the asking, and if one uses the best, in even over-generous quantities, one gets a lovely wine for about 1s 6d a bottle. This being so, why bother to produce a beverage for fourpence a bottle which is no more like wine than the Common Market is like Petticoat Lane?

I make wine—not country wine . . . I make real wine, not a sort of alcoholic drink that's a type of wine-like wine that's like wine.

Are my fellow winemakers poverty-stricken? Must they scour the countryside for rubbish that even the animals won't eat? Let's put aside our Wellingtons and buy for our ingredients the fruits that man has discovered, after centuries of experiment, are good to eat.

JEFFREY ROBINSON, KINGSBURY, IN A LETTER TO A.W.

★   ★   ★

Counsellor

I can truthfully say that since I reached the age of discretion I have consistently drunk more than most people would say was good for me. Nor do I regret it. Wine has been to me a firm friend and a wise counsellor. Often wine has shown me matters in their true perspective, and has, as though by the touch of a magic wand, reduced great disasters to small inconveniences. DUFF COOPER: OLD MEN FORGET.

"*I wish you'd ease up on that wood alcohol, Bill!*"

Water Risk

I was once told by that great but eccentric specialist in longevity, Dr. Julien Besancon, that wine, not water, should be regarded as the natural drink of man, and that water was a dangerous poison. I was pleased, but surprised, and pointed out that water was what all animals on earth normally drink. To this the doctor replied "Yes, and they die of it" and pointed out that man was the smallest consumer of water among mammals of comparable size and the longest lived of them all. Beer, he said, was at least better than water, tea or coffee, all of which he condemned as most unwholesome. Nor did he approve of spirits, excepting perhaps a mouthful of very good brandy after a meal.

EDWARD HYAMS: VIN.

★ ★ ★

Church Ales

To drink well, means also to drink with understanding, and to drink with understanding does not mean to drink wantonly. The lie to that is given by all the old parish churches in England. With our background of prejudice against a rational life it is curious to ponder on these old buildings, examples of devotion, good fellowship and beauty such as few countries possess, and then to remember that those beautiful old churches of East Anglia, for instance, which rise up like cathedrals in the quiet English countryside, were maintained and partly built out of the profits of the "Church Ales" . . . In the Tudor period these Church Ales were usually held on Sundays. A practice which would be considered as shocking as the drinking of ale at a religious festival.

G. R. GAYRE: WASSAIL.

Screen Test

It is important to realise that the Road Safety Act does not suggest that a driver is drunk when his blood alcohol level exceeds 80 mg per 100 ml: it merely states that it is an offence to drive when the level is above this statutory limit. In this respect the law governing drinking is exactly analogous to that concerned with speeding and driving. The law does not question the competence of the driver who exceeds the speed limit; it only states that when he does so he commits an offence.

Under the present law a driver can only be asked to take a breath test by a police officer in uniform and only if the officer suspects him of having alcohol in his body or of having committed a traffic offence while the vehicle was in motion.

No driver can, however, be convicted on the result of a breath test alone. It is merely a screening test and no great accuracy is claimed for it.

ADVICE IN "WINE MINE".

★ ★ ★

Alcohol is not the direct cause of any known disease, and there is none that it will cure.

RICHARD SERJEANT: A MAN MAY DRINK.

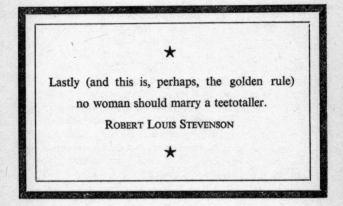

Lastly (and this is, perhaps, the golden rule)
no woman should marry a teetotaller.

Robert Louis Stevenson

CHAPTER THIRTEEN

THE
SIGNAL-ROD

�֍

Winemaker's Bible

If someone mentioned the "Winemaker's Bible" to you, you would probably think of "First Steps in Winemaking" and not of the Holy Bible. The New English Bible . . . gives the phrase a different slant.

One thing—it is plain that winemakers could not have a more exalted patron. Here is how the New English Bible describes how Jesus produced somewhere between seven hundred and a thousand bottles of the best wine for the wedding-feast in the house in Cana-in-Galilee.

"There were six stone water jars standing near, of the kind used for Jewish rites of purification; each held from twenty to thirty gallons. Jesus said to the servants "Fill the jars with water" and they filled them to the brim. "Now draw off some" he ordered "and take it to the steward of the feast"; and they did so.

The steward tasted the water now turned into wine, not knowing its source: though the servants who had drawn the water knew. He hailed the bridegroom and said: "Everybody serves the best wine first and waits until the guests have drunk freely before serving the poorer sort: but you have kept the best wine until now".

This was not the normal way of making wine in Biblical times! Normally the grapes were picked when ripe and (sometimes after having been laid in the sun to concentrate the juice) were thrown into a stone vat cut where possible out of the solid rock. There they were thoroughly trampled underfoot, the juice running away down a channel to another vat cut in the rock further downhill. When the grapes had been trampled they were usually pressed, sometimes under heavy weights or under a beam with one end set in a notch in the rock for leverage.

The wine was left in the lower vat for six weeks to settle and ferment. Usually in the heat of Palastine fermentation was complete at the end of this time. If the vat was needed for a second pressing before the six weeks were up, the first batch was drawn off into jars and racked regularly to get rid of the lees.

It was drunk diluted with as much as two parts of water to one of wine—about the alcoholic strength of pub beer.

Most winemakers, coming on the text in Isaiah about "a feast of fat things, a feast of wine on the lees" would be inclined to gag and shudder, thinking of the way in which wine left too long on its sediment becomes off-flavoured as the yeast breaks down, with little pock-marked craters appearing on the smooth surface of the sediment. But this text, in the new translation, squares better with modern techniques. "A banquet of wines well matured and richest fare, well matured and strained clear". Those who make a regular practice of filtering their wines can quote Scripture to back them up: I take it for granted that we all mature our wines: as the Apocrypha says "A new friend is like a new wine: you do not enjoy drinking it until it has matured".

When the lover in the "Song of Solomon" says "Your love is more fragrant than wine" we know that he is speaking of a wine with bouquet. We'd all approve of that, even though we do not always achieve it. But what about "Wine that foams in the cup, hot with spice"? Not to the taste of the modern winemaker, though it isn't so many years since the average home-made wine in Britain was inevitably (and sometimes mercifully) spiced.

We've all met the enthusiast (often confident in his prowess) whose wine fits the description "the poison of dragons". That's how the Authorised Version describes it, and the new translation is no more complimentary.—"Their wine is the venom of serpents, the poison of asps". Can't imagine one like that reaching the prize-list in even a local show, let alone the National.

You can search the book without finding any approval of drunkenness. Wine is to be enjoyed, as well as being the symbol of joy, of life, of blood, and at last of the Covenant which is celebrated in Communion and the Mass.

The famous "Look not thou upon the wine when it is red, when it giveth his colour in the cup . . . at the last it biteth like the serpent and stingeth like an adder" is even more vivid in the new translation. You'd swear that the writer of Proverbs knew what a good-going hangover was like.

"Whose is the misery? Whose the remorse? Where are the quarrels and the anxiety? Who gets the bruises without knowing why? Those who linger later over their wine, those who are always trying some new spiced liquor. Do not gulp down the wine, the strong red wine, when the droplets form on the side of the cup. In the end it will bite like a snake and sting like a cobra. Then your eyes see strange sights, like one who clings to the top of the rigging. You say 'If it lays me flat, what do I care? If it brings me to the ground, what of it? As soon as I wake up I shall turn to it again'."

Maybe it was the same writer, speaking from bitter experience, who said "Wine is a mocker, strong drink is a raging . . ." or as it now appears, "Wine is an insolent fellow, and strong drink makes an uproar. No-one addicted to their company grows wise."

"Don't drink too much" is excellent advice in any

generation; and home brewers and wine-makers could also follow the example of the king who gave the feast described in the Book of Esther". ". . . and the law of the drinking was that there should be no compulsion, for the king had laid it down that all the stewards of the palace should respect each man's wishes". A lesson to the enthusiasts who, when their guests are already sloshing around gill-deep in wine and beer, insist "You must try my 1969 Celandine and Hemlock Malmsey" and dish out half-tumblers-ful.

Sometimes the words lose in translation. The beautiful "Go thy way, eat thy bread with joy and drink thy wine with a merry heart, for God now accepteth thy works" is more accurate perhaps but loses its ring when it becomes "Go to it then, eat your food and enjoy it, and drink your wine with a cheerful heart, for already God has accepted what you have done". And who would want to change "Like the best wine, for my beloved, that goeth down sweetly, causing the lips of those that are asleep to speak" for "And your whispers like spiced wine, flowing smoothly to welcome my caresses, gliding down through lips and teeth".

Amateur winemakers can take it that those texts refer also to wines made from other ingredients than grapes and grape concentrate, for the Jews (like ourselves) used dates and apples, as well as pomegranates.   DUNCAN GILLESPIE IN A.W.

It was a miracle divine
Which turned water into wine.
Alas that man through grief and pain
Should have to turn it back again!

SEEN BY PAUL JENTS ON WALL AT A WINE TASTING.

Patroness of Mead

There are also connections between mead and the famous and popular St. Brigit, who, as Our Lord turned water into wine, changed vats of water into mead, and, even, on one occasion did something more remarkable, when the King of Leinster came to drink the mead prepared for him it could not be found. Whereupon St. Brigit, equal to the occasion, blessed the empty vessels which immediately filled with mead.

G. R. GAYRE: WASSAIL!

★ ★ ★

Wine drunken with moderation is the joy of the soul, and the heart. Wine drunken with excess raiseth quarrels and wraths and many ruins.

ECCLESIASTICUS, CHAP. XXXL.

★ ★ ★

All-Father's Guests

Gangler asked (no doubt with some concern) if water was drunk in Valhalla, and Thor, in answer, re-assured him by asking if he believed that Kings and Earls would be invited by the All-father to drink only water! Men who had suffered great hardships, wounds and pain, even unto death, to reach Valhalla would have paid too great a price, if water was their mead. No, from the goat Laerath there flowed such plenteous mead that the heroes were fully satisfied of it.

The Celts also held to much the same view, for in their paradise there was a river of mead at which those who had won through to immortality could refresh themselves.

These ideas of hearty Norseman and Celt were a trifle different, as touching the Diety's hospitality, than is to be found in some of the teetotal tracts.

WASSAIL!

The Ageless Mystery

We call on You, O Barley Mother
We who brew by day and night
Working with Your golden bounty
May our worts run clear and bright.

Though man builds as high as mountains,
And rides the sky on wings of flame,
Yet the Springtime and the Harvest
Will for ever be the same.

For all our science and our wonders,
All our sweat and all our pain,
Yet we really aren't so clever,
We cannot make a single grain.

We call on You, O Barley Mother,
As once with mint, but now with hops
Working with Your golden bounty
We may not waste those precious drops.

KEN SHALES: ADVANCED HOME BREWING.

★ ★ ★

Mother's Milk

The Indians of Tecospa, then, are traditionalists, and they are wedded to the land. This land, besides producing maize, beans and squash, produces the maguey plant from which they make pulque, their native intoxicant. From pre-Conquest times to the present, pulque has been considered a holy beverage —"the milk of our mother" (the Virgin) as they now put it—and an integral part of Tecospan life from conception to the hereafter . . . despite the high degree of intoxication the Tecospans achieve, when they drink among themselves, the sharing of pulque symbolises social and spiritual brotherhood, and violence is unheard of. DRUNKEN COMPORTMENT.

Elder Brother

It seems that one day Elder Brother, their deity, noticed the dryness of their soil and decided to remedy the situation. He placed beads of his perspiration in the ground and circled the spot in ceremonial fashion for four days, at the end of which time a saguaro cactus had sprouted, grown to its full stature, and borne fruit. Elder Brother took this fruit, mixed its juice with water, and said "Let me see if we cannot make rain with this to refresh the thirsty soil". With this (the myth continues) the mixture became wine, and rain began to fall. Thus, it is held, did the Papago learn to make wine from the fruit of the saguaro; and thus, too, did they come to learn that by drinking this wine in annual religious ceremony they achieved the power to "pull down the clouds", thereby ensuring their survival for yet another year . . .

"The young dandies reddened the soles of their feet so that when they fell over, drunk, the beautiful colour would show."

C. MacAndrew and R. B. Edgerton: Drunken Comportment.

★　　★　　★

Hail Bacchus! hail thou peaceful God of Wine
Hail Bacchus Hail! Here comes thy darling vine
Drunk with her own rich juice, she cannot stand
But comes supported by her husband's hand;
The lusty elm supports her stagg'ring tree
My best belov'd plant, how I am charmed with thee!

Abraham Cowley.

"*Honestly Mabel — you're enough to drive a man to drink!*"

Passion-Fruit

A . . . proposition for the wine-maker with a south
wall is the passion-fruit. It gets its name from the
Passion of Christ, for the flower was used as a
parable by the missionaries—the five stamens repre-
sented the five wounds, the three stigmas the three
nails, the style of the pistil the column at which
Christ was flogged, the corona His crown of thorns,
the fingered leaves the hands of the multitude, the
coiled tendrils the flogging cords and the five sepals
and the five petals the faithful disciples (excluding
Judas and Peter). Though it comes from South
Brazil, passiflora caerulea is more or less hardy on a
south wall, and makes a handsome almost evergreen
plant. It grows quickly in a good soil. The fruits are
egg-sized and egg-shaped; the plant will still be
flowering in the autumn, and full of the buzz of late
bees, when you gather them. Pruning consists of
pruning back the side-shoots to a short stub, to
encourage new shoots to grow and replace old
wood.

DUNCAN GILLESPIE: THE WINEMAKER'S GARDEN.

CHAPTER FOURTEEN

NOT SO THINK AS . . .

Drunk

Everybody knows the meaning of this word as applied to those who have over-indulged in alcoholic beverages, but there is no satisfactory scientific definition, although there are over 1400 synonyms in English alone for the term. Incidentally, the next candidate for the honour is Finland with over 600 synonyms. In English, and apparently also in many other languages, there are few censorious synonyms for drunk. The overwhelming majority of the terms are good-natured, tolerant, amusing. The moral should be clear.

THE DICTIONARY OF DRINK AND DRINKING.

★ ★ ★

"If any monk through drinking too freely gets thick of speech so that he cannot join in the psalms he is to be deprived of his supper".

THE MONK GILDAS, AROUND 540 AD.

★ ★ ★

First to go

There is a popular idea that alcohol is a stimulant to all mental process. This is because with alcohol the first part of the brain to be depressed is the front part controlling caution, hesitation, self-criticism and self-judgement. These are the inhibitions of society and in many tasks those characteristics are a hindrance rather than a help—after-dinner speaking, examinations, etc.

DR. B. FINCH: PASSPORT TO PARADISE?

Rotary Motion

After two pints the wife led me gently to the bath-room where I cast my bread upon the waters, and then to bed where I clung to the sheets until all rotary motion ceased . . .

Another night that will live long in my memory was a Federation gathering at York. We had a marvellous time, but as we were leaving the building I had to wait in the foyer for the rest of our group, when suddenly I felt the whole place give a distinct lurch and start swaying. Being a brave lad, I got my back up against the wall and this held it fairly steady until all our group were out. Then I made a dash for the doorway. It was about twelve feet wide when we came in, but now I had removed my support it must have been collapsing because both doorposts hit my shoulders as I went through. I dare not look back in case I got the blame. (Incidentally, not one person in our circle even thanked me for my heroic deed, and the papers never even mentioned any falling build-ings. Funny, that!)

J. DIXON, RECALLING "PERFECTLY TRUE HAPPENINGS"
IN A.W.

★   ★   ★

But I'm not so think as you drunk I am!

SIR JOHN SQUIRES.

143

Full of Joy

"He drank seven times. His thoughts wandered. He became hilarious. His heart was full of joy and his face shone".

DESCRIPTION OF THE REACTION OF THE SAVAGE ENKIDU WHEN HE FIRST TASTED DATE WINE. EPIC OF GILGAMISH.

★　★　★

One Roman drinker to another, the morning after, "Are you Appius Claudius?" "No, I'm as miserable as sin".

TOLD BY CEDRIC AUSTIN IN A.W.

★　★　★

Sottism

"Take not upon thyself to drink a jug of beer. Thou speakest, and an unintelligible utterance issueth from thy mouth. If thou fallest down and thy limbs break, there is none to hold out a hand to thee. Thy companions in drink stand up and say "Away with this sot". If there then cometh one to seek thee in order to question thee, thou art found lying on the ground and art like a little child".

WRITTEN IN EGYPT, 1000 BC AND QUOTED IN "A MAN MAY DRINK", RICHARD SERGEANT ADDING THE COMMENT "THINGS DO NOT APPEAR TO HAVE CHANGED MUCH; NOTE THE REGRETTABLE CALLOUSNESS OF ONE'S FRIENDS IN THE IMPLICIT PROXIMITY OF THE LAW".

"*Now then — what'll you have?*"

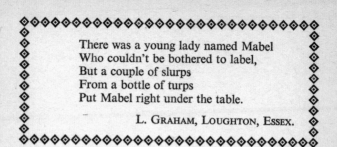

There was a young lady named Mabel
Who couldn't be bothered to label,
But a couple of slurps
From a bottle of turps
Put Mabel right under the table.

L. GRAHAM, LOUGHTON, ESSEX.

Not Just Fun

The European who sees a Nandi continually getting drunk, although he is at the same time short of food, does not realise that beer is a social necessity and not merely an enjoyment. If a Nandi cannot from time to time give a beer party, even a small party, he will lose social standing; he will be considered mean, and will not be asked by his neighbours to partake of beer. He will be, unofficially but none the less effectively, pushed out of his rightful place in the *koret*, i.e., parish. COLONIAL RESEARCH STUDIES.

CHAPTER FIFTEEN

WISE AND OTHERWISE

�֍

Winged Words

"Teetotalism gives a man wings to fly, a tongue to speak, feet to walk, eyes to see, in a word gives liberty to breathe. Who can describe the blessings of teetotalism?"

PRESTON TEMPERANCE ADVOCATE, JULY, 1836.

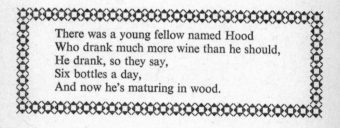

There was a young fellow named Hood
Who drank much more wine than he should,
He drank, so they say,
Six bottles a day,
And now he's maturing in wood.

Degradation of Drunkenness. There is no sin which doth more deface God's image than drunkenness. It disguiseth a person and doth even unman him. Drunkenness makes him have the throat of a fish, the belly of a swine, and the head of an ass. Drunkenness is the sham of nature, the extinguisher of reason, the shipwreck of chastity and the murderer of conscience. Drunkenness is hurtful to the body, the cup kills more than the cannon, it causes dropsies, catarrhs, apoplexies, it fills the eye with fire and the legs with water and turns the body into an hospital.
FROM A STONE TABLET OUTSIDE THE VICARAGE,

KINDFORD, SUSSEX.

Cheese it

The Cardiff and District Temperance Council say that adding beer to cheese "only makes the task of the Council which tries to protect the young from drink more difficult". How much of this lascivious cheese do you eat to become affected. Well, there's one pint of beer in 20lb of cheese so work it out for yourselves. Good eating.

E. A. ROYCROFT IN A.W.

A winemaker, slightly hilarious,
Mixed all of his wines, which were various;
Then drank them, unaided—
He's now quite persuaded
He's really Archbishop Makarios.

F. R. CANNING, DOVER N.J., U.S.A., IN A.W.

The more's the pity, I must say
That so many men and women are by it led astray,
And decoyed from the paths of virtue and led on to vice
By drinking too much alcohol and acting unwise.

WILLIAM McGONAGALL.

★　★　★

How can I, who drink good wine and bitter beer every day of my life, coolly stand up and advise hard-working fellow-creatures to take the pledge?

WILLIAM EWART GLADSTONE, PRIME MINISTER.

Temperance

Next to patriotism, this is probably the most abused word in the English language. Instead of meaning of reasonable or of moderate usage, it has been corrupted to become a synonym of total abstinence from alcoholic beverages. A temperance hotel is thus the very opposite to its face meaning. The truly temperate people are not the teetotallers but the moderate drinkers of light wines and ales with food and the imbibers of small alcoholic appetisers with tit-bits of food before meals.

THE DICTIONARY OF DRINK AND DRINKING.

> The rich man has a cellar,
> And a ready butler by him;
> The poor must steer
> For his pint of beer
> Where the saint can't choose but spy him.
>
> THOMAS LOVE PEACOCK.

Water-drinkers are universally laughed at; but, it has always seemed to me, that they are amongst the most welcome of guests, and that too, though the host be by no means of a niggardly turn. The truth is, they give no trouble; they occasion no anxiety to please them; they are sure not to make their sittings inconveniently long; and, which is the great thing of all, their example teaches moderation to the rest of the company . . .

WILLIAM COBBETT: ADVICE TO A YOUTH.

★　★　★

The process of manufacture, or what may more properly be called the process of destruction of valuable grain by malting and brewing, is as follows—

THE WORSHIP OF BACCHUS A GREAT DELUSION, 1876.

Time Gentlemen, Please!

ACKNOWLEDGEMENT

AS compiler of "Full to the Bung" I must acknowledge with gratitude the many hours of pleasure I have found in reading the "Amateur Winemaker", the books written by my fellow-authors in the A.W. stable, and the books and publications listed below.

My thanks, and that of the publishers of this book, are due to many people for their co-operation in granting permission (in almost every case freely) to quote interesting informative and amusing extracts.

The principal books quoted, other than those published by A.W., are listed here under their publishers' names— Allen and Unwin, "Drugs, Medicine and Man" by Harold Brown. Cassell, "Encyclopaedia of Wines and Spirits" by Alexis Lichine. Chatto and Windus, "Another Kind of Magic" by Mollie Harris. Dennis Dobson, "From Barrel to Bottle" by Edward Ott. Duckworth & Co., "Wine's My Line" by T. A. Layton. English University Press, "Teach Yourself Wine" by R. S. Don. Faber & Faber Ltd., "Suffolk Prospect" by Justin and Edith Brooke; "Winemaking for All" and "Beermaking for All" by James Macgregor; and "Amateur Winemaking" by S. M. Tritton. Granada Pubns., "Passport to Paradise?" by Dr. Bernard Finch; "Food Facts and Fallacies" by Fredericks and Bailey; and "Wine Growing in England" by George Ordish. G. G. Harrap, "Green Medicine" by M. B. Kreig. Wm. Heinemann Ltd., "The Inheritors" by Ritchie Calder; and " A Song for Every Season" by Bob Copper. M. & J. Hobbs, "Eat, Drink and be Sorry" by Andre Launey. Hutchison, "The Drugs You Take" by Dr. S. Bradshaw. International Wine and Food Pubn. Co., "Gods, Men and Wine" by William Younger. Michael Joseph Ltd., "Stay me with Flagons" by Maurice Healey. MacMillan, London and Basingstoke, "Dictionary of Drink and Drinking" by Oscar A. Mendelsohn. Methuen, "In a Glass Lightly" by Cyril Ray. Mills and Boon, "Winemakers Companion" by B. C. A. Turner and C. J. J. Berry; and "Simple Guide to Home Made Beer" by B. C. A. Turner and D. J. Moon. Thos. Nelson and Sons, "Wine" by Hugh Johnson and "Drunken Comportment" by C. McAndrew and R. Edgerton. Newnes, "Vin" by Edward

Hyams. Odhams "Country Wines" by Mary Aylett. Pelham Books, "AB-Z of Winemaking" by B. C. A. Turner. Penguin Books Ltd., "Penguin Book of Wines" (1965), p. 40 by Allan Sichel; and "Wines and Spirits" (1957) p. 270 by L. W. Marrison. Putnam and Co., "A Man May Drink" by Richard Sergeant. Routledge and Kegan Paul, "Beverage Report" by Derek Cooper. Charles Scribner's Sons, "Guide to Wine, Spirits and Beers" 4th Rev. Edn., by Harold J. Grossman. Souvenir Press, "Omnivore" by Dr. Lyall Watson. Wine and Spirit Publications, "Wine Tasting" by J. M. Broadbent.

Many other books, long out of print, are also quoted from (and acknowledged) in the text, as are several brief passages from Peter Dominic's catalogue-magazine "Wine Mine".

DUNCAN GILLESPIE.

Other "AW" Books

FIRST STEPS IN WINEMAKING

The acknowledged introduction to the subject. Unbeatable at the price.

C. J. J. Berry   35p, p. & p. 8p

SCIENTIFIC WINEMAKING—made easy

The most advanced and practical textbook on the subject.

J. R. Mitchell, L.I.R.C., A.I.F.S.T.

Paperback 60p, p. & p. 9p
Hard cover 90p. p. & p. 11p

THE WINEMAKER'S COOKBOOK

Gives a whole range of exciting dishes using your home-made wine.

Tilly Timbrell and Bryan Acton   35p, p. & p. 6p

WINEMAKING AND BREWING

The theory and practice of winemaking and brewing in detail.

Dr. F. W. Beech and Dr. A. Pollard   35p, p. & p. 8p

GROWING GRAPES IN BRITAIN

Indispensable handbook for winemakers whether they have six vines or six thousand.

Gillian Pearkes   35p, p. & p. 8p

"AMATEUR WINEMAKER" RECIPES

Fascinatingly varied collection of over 200 recipes.

C. J. J. Berry   35p, p. & p. 7p

WINEMAKING WITH CANNED AND DRIED FRUIT

How to make delightful wines from off the supermarket shelf.

C. J. J. Berry   35p, p. & p. 6p

PRESERVING WINEMAKING INGREDIENTS

Includes drying, chunk bottling, deep freezing, chemical preservation, etc.

T. Edwin Belt   35p, p. & p. 6p

LIGHTHEARTED SPEECHMAKING
—To assure anyone who has to speak in public.
Duncan Gillespie   40p, p. & p. 6p

PROGRESSIVE WINEMAKING
500 pages, from scientific theory to the production of quality wines at home.
Peter Duncan and Bryan Acton   Paperback 75p, p. & p. 14p
Hard cover £1.25, p. & p. 19p

HOME BREWED BEERS AND STOUTS
The first and still recognised as the best book on this fascinating subject.
C. J. J. Berry   30p, p. & p. 6p

WOODWORK FOR WINEMAKERS
Make your own wine press, fermentation cupboard, fruit pulper, bottle racks, etc.
C. J. Dart and D. A. Smith   35p, p. & p. 6p

BREWING BETTER BEERS
Explains many finer points of brewing technique.
Ken Shales   35p, p. & p. 6p

HINTS ON HOME BREWING
Concise and basic down to earth instructions on home brewing.
C. J. J. Berry   15p, p. & p. 5p

MAKING MEAD
The only full-length paperback available on this winemaking speciality.
Bryan Acton and Peter Duncan   35p, p. & p. 6p

LIGHTHEARTED WINEMAKING
Instructional in a lighthearted way.
Duncan Gillespie   35p, p. & p. 6p

THE WINEMAKER'S RECITER
For the winemaker with a sense of humour.
Philip Delmon   50p, p. & p. 6p

PLANTS UNSAFE FOR WINEMAKING
—includes native and naturalised plants, shrubs and trees.
T. Edwin Belt   40p, p. & p. 6p

GROWING VINES
Down-to-earth book for the viticulturalist.
N. Poulter   35p, p. & p. 6p

DURDEN PARK BEER CIRCLE BOOK OF RECIPES
How to make a whole range of superb beers.
Wilf Newsom   25p, p. & p. 4p

JUDGING HOME-MADE WINES
National Guild of Judges official handbook.   25p, p. & p. 4p

BINDERS
De luxe binders for your copies of the *Amateur Winemaker*
                                    80p, p. & p. 14p

WINEMAKERS' AND BREWERS' TIES
Two patterns, both maroon background
Single golden goblet   ⎱   £1·36 incl. VAT and
Overall pattern of tiny golden goblets   ⎰   postage
VINTAGE pattern £1·69 incl. VAT and postage.
BREWERS' pattern £1·69 incl. VAT and postage.

WINE CARDS
Recipes for superb commercial type wines.
C. J. J. Berry   39p per pack, p. & p. 6p

BEER CARDS
Recipes for excellent beers, from lager to double stout.
C. J. J. Berry   39p per pack, p. & p. 6p

WINERY CARD
The most useful card ever produced for the winemaker.
                         Only 10p, p. & p. 3p

WINE LOG
For recording all your winemaking.
         Cover with 25 cards 71p, (incl. VAT) p. & p. 10p
         Cover with 50 cards 86p. (incl. VAT) p. & p. 12p
         25 cards 16p. (incl. VAT) p. & p. 4p
         100 cards 55p. (incl. VAT) p. & p. 10p.